Religion 1
for Young Catholics

THE SETON CATHOLIC FAMILY CATECHISM SERIES

(A RELIGION SERIES FOR CHILDREN EDUCATED AT HOME BY THEIR PARENTS)

D1636914

Seton Press
Front Royal, Virginia

Executive Editor: Dr. Mary Kay Clark

Seton Press
1350 Progress Drive
Front Royal, VA 22630

(540) 636-9990 phone
(540) 636-1602 fax

Internet: http://www.setonpress.com
E-mail: info@setonpress.com

Cover: *Madonna and Child*, Bartolomé Esteban Murillo

Dedicated to the Sacred Heart of Jesus

We thank Jesus in His Most Sacred Heart for directing our writing, editing, illustrating, and desktop publishing. We thank His Most Blessed Mother Mary, and His father on earth, St. Joseph, both of whom were perfect parents who taught their perfect Son, Jesus, at home.

Published with Ecclesiastical Permission
Diocese of Arlington
May 16, 1997

Foreword

Religion 1 for Young Catholics will help teach children at the First Grade level about their Catholic Faith. Children at this grade level cannot be expected to read the lessons by themselves. The teaching parent will need to read and discuss the lessons for the child.

Seton Home Study School is following the directives of the General Catechetical Directory from the Vatican, as well as the new Catechism of the Catholic Church. Both the Directory and the new Catechism emphasize the importance of teaching all of the basic truths of the Faith each year: the Creed, the Commandments, the Sacraments, and the Prayers. At the same time, the Directory states that the lessons are to be presented at a level appropriate for the age of the child.

Organization of the Text

The text-workbook consists of lessons distributed over thirty-six weeks. Four lessons are to be covered in the course of the week. With children of this age, fifteen or twenty minutes per lesson should be enough time.

Four review units are included for Week Nine, Eighteen, Twenty-Seven and Thirty-Six. Some of the review questions found on Day 4 of each week may be preceded by an asterisk. The asterisk indicates that the question and answer are taken directly from the Baltimore Catechism.

While all the Sacraments and all the Commandments are taught in this text, the authors have tried to present lessons with an appropriate vocabulary and short sentences as much as possible.

This text is used in the Seton Home Study School curriculum. Enrolled students are sent supplemental materials, such as the First Communion edition of the Baltimore Catechism. Non-enrolled families may contact Seton to purchase additional supplemental materials. The many educational materials available can be seen at www.setonbooks.com.

Contents

QUARTER 2   WEEK - DAY

QUARTER 3   WEEK - DAY

QUARTER 4   WEEK - DAY

Sign of the Cross

In the Name of the Father,
and of the Son,
and of the Holy Spirit. Amen.

The Glory Be to the Father

Glory be to the Father,
and to the Son,
and to the Holy Spirit,
as it was in the beginning,
is now,
and ever shall be,
world without end. Amen

God in Heaven

Prayer to my Guardian Angel

Angel of God,
my guardian dear,
to whom God's Love
entrusts me here.
Ever this day
be at my side,
to light, to guard,
to rule, to guide. Amen.

My Guardian Angel watches over me.

Short Prayers

All for Jesus through Mary.

My Jesus, mercy!

Most Sacred Heart of Jesus, have mercy on us.

Immaculate Heart of Mary,
pray for us now and at the hour of our death. Amen.

Most Sacred Heart of Jesus,
I will continue to perform all my actions for the love of Thee. Amen.

Jesus in my heart, I believe in Your love for me. I love You.

Jesus, Mary, and Joseph, I love you, save souls.

Jesus, Mary, and Joseph

The Hail Mary

Hail Mary, full of Grace,
the Lord is with thee.
Blessed art thou among women,
and blessed is the Fruit of thy womb,
Jesus.
Holy Mary, Mother of God,
pray for us sinners
now and at the hour of our death. Amen.

The Lord's Prayer

Our Father, Who art in Heaven,
hallowed be Thy Name.
Thy Kingdom come,
Thy Will be done on earth
as it is in Heaven.
Give us this day our daily Bread.
And forgive us our trespasses
as we forgive those
who trespass against us.
And lead us not into temptation,
but deliver us from evil. Amen.

The Annunciation

An Act of Contrition

O my God, I am heartily sorry
for having offended Thee.
And I detest all my sins,
because I dread the loss of Heaven
and the pains of hell.
But most of all because they offend Thee, my God,
Who art all good and deserving of all my love.
I firmly resolve, with the help of Thy Grace,
to confess my sins, to do penance,
and to amend my life. Amen

The Crucifixion

The Apostles' Creed

I believe in God, the Father Almighty,
Creator of Heaven and earth,

And in Jesus Christ, His only Son, our Lord,

Who was conceived by the Holy Spirit,
born of the Virgin Mary,

Suffered under Pontius Pilate,
was crucified, died, and was buried.

He descended into hell; the third day He
arose again from the dead.

He ascended into Heaven, and sits at the
right hand of God, the Father Almighty.

From thence He shall come to judge the
living and the dead.

I believe in the Holy Spirit,

the Holy Catholic Church, the Communion
of Saints,

the forgiveness of sins,

the resurrection of the body,

and life everlasting. Amen.

Blessing Before Meals

Bless us, O Lord,
And these Thy gifts,
Which we are about to receive
from Thy bounty,
Through Christ our Lord. Amen

Blessing After Meals

We give Thee thanks
Almighty God,
for these and all Thy benefits,
which we have received,
from Thy bounty
through Christ, Our Lord. Amen
May the souls of the faithful departed,
through the mercy of God,
rest in peace. Amen.

Miraculous Catch of Fishes

Prayer

What is prayer?

   Prayer is the lifting up of our minds and hearts to God.

Why do we pray?

   We pray for several reasons:

   1. to adore God;
   2. to thank God for all He has given us;
   3. to ask pardon for our sins;
   4. to ask for graces and blessings for ourselves and for others.

Madonna and Child adored by saints

God Our Father

God knows all things.
God knows all things in Heaven and on the earth.
God knows what happened in the past.
God knows what is happening now.
God knows what will happen in the future.
God knows what we do and say.
God even knows what we think.

God watches over us and takes care of us.
God can do anything.
He can make anything or change anything.
Most of all, He loves us and helps us.
He loves us and helps us when we pray to Him.

God is all good.
God is always true.

The Trinity in Heaven

God Our Father

We believe in God, the Father Almighty.
God is our loving Father in Heaven.
God made us.
God made us because He loves us.
We love God because He made us.
He made us to live someday with Him in Heaven.

God our Father is with us on earth.
However, we cannot see Him now.
God is a pure spirit, without a body.
But we will see Him in Heaven.
Heaven is God's home.
Someday, when we die, Heaven will be our home too.

God never had a beginning.
Everything we see had a beginning.
The world had a beginning.
The animals had a beginning.
You and I had a beginning.
Everything and everyone we see on the earth had a beginning.
Even things we don't see, like the Angels, had a beginning.
But God had no beginning.

God the Father was not created, made, or born.
God always was and God always will be.
This is a great mystery which we will understand better in Heaven.

Things we see on earth die or end.
The grass dies each year. Flowers and trees die each year.
But God always was, and always will be. God always stays the same.
God loves us and will always love us. God will always watch over us.
God will always do what is best for us.

God Our Father

There is only one God.
In God, there are three Divine Persons.
We call this the Blessed Trinity.

Each time you make the Sign of the Cross,
you greet the Most Blessed Trinity.

God the Father is the first Person of the Blessed Trinity.
God the Son is Jesus Christ, the second Person of the Blessed Trinity.
God the Holy Spirit is the third Person of the Blessed Trinity.

There is only one God.
In God, there are three Divine Persons:
the Father,
the Son,
and the Holy Spirit.

God in Heaven

We call the three Divine Persons in one
God the Blessed Trinity.
We know there are three Divine Persons in
one God
because Jesus is God and He told us all
about God.

There are three families that are important
to me.
The first family important to me is my family on earth:
my father and my mother, my brothers and sisters,
my grandparents, my aunts, uncles, and relatives.

Another family important to me is the Holy Family:
Jesus, Mary, and Joseph.

A third family important to me is the Trinity of God:
God the Father, God the Son, and God the Holy Spirit.

God Our Father

Who is God?

God is our Father in Heaven Who made us.

Where is God?

God is everywhere.

Does God know all things?

Yes, God knows all things.

Can God do all things?

Yes, God can do all things.

Did God have a beginning?

No, God had no beginning. He always was.

The Coronation of Our Lady as Queen of Heaven

Will God always be?

Yes, God will always be.

Does God watch over us?

Yes, God always will love us and watch over us.

God and Creation

God is the Creator.
There is only one Creator.
God is the Creator.
God is the Creator because He created all things out of nothing.

When we make something, we must use something to make it.
If we make a wagon, we need wood and wheels.
If we make a cake, we need the cake mix, eggs, and milk.

God is the one and only true Creator.
He makes all things out of nothing.
We call God's power to make things out of nothing
His power to create.

God is our Creator.
God created each one of our souls out of nothing.
God created each Angel out of nothing.

God is the Creator of all things.
God created each separate kind of animal and plant.
God created all things visible and invisible out of nothing.

Creation

God and Creation

God had no beginning.
God said: "I Am Who Am."
God always was and always will be forever and ever.
God is so great and so good that nothing exists without Him.

In the beginning, God created Heaven and earth.
God created invisible spiritual things first.
He created the Angels to be with Him.
God created the Angels to share His happiness in Heaven.
Then God created the visible material universe.

God had a wonderful plan.
And because God knows and can do all things,
His plan included you and your parents
and all the things He created from the very beginning.

Long ago, God told holy men about how He created the earth.
The holy men wrote the story of God's creation in the Bible.
The Bible is a holy book.
The first chapter of the Bible tells the story of Creation.

God created the material universe.

God and Creation

In the beginning, God created heaven and earth. The earth was void and empty and dark, and the spirit of God breathed over the waters. Then God created light and separated it from the darkness. And God called the light Day and the darkness Night and that was the first day of Creation.

On the second day, God made a firmament or space to divide the waters above it from the waters below it and He called the space Heaven.

On the third day, God commanded the land and the oceans and the seas to form. God called the dry land Earth and the waters He called seas. God saw that it was good. Then God commanded the earth to bring forth living, green plants with seeds so that each plant could reproduce others like itself from its own seeds, and fruit trees bearing fruits with seeds in them which when planted would grow other fruit trees each like itself.

On the fourth day, God created the sun and moon, and stars to rule the day and the night, to divide the light and the darkness, and to be signs marking time and seasons.

On the fifth day, God created the great whales and every living and moving creature which the waters brought forth according to their kinds, and every winged bird according to its kind. God saw that it was good. He blessed each new creature, saying: Increase and multiply and fill the waters of the sea; and let the birds be multiplied upon the earth.

On the sixth day, God created all kinds of animals from the earth, cattle and creeping things, and beasts of the earth, according to their kinds. And then God said, "Let us make man to Our image and likeness. And let him be in charge of the fishes of the sea and the birds of the air, and the animals, and the whole earth and every creeping creature that moves on the earth." And then God created the first man, Adam. But Adam did not find a companion like himself among the animals of the earth so God created and gave Adam his wife Eve, the first woman. God blessed Adam and Eve saying: Increase and multiply, and fill the earth, and subdue it, and rule over the fishes of the sea, and the birds of the air, and all the living creatures that move upon the earth.

God and Creation

Who created you?

God created me.

Did God create all things?

Yes, God created all things.

Did God create the Angels?

Yes, God created the Angels.

Garden of Eden

Did God make the sun, moon, and stars?

Yes, God made the sun, moon, and stars.

Did God make the land and the seas on the earth?

Yes, God made the land and the seas on the earth.

Did God make many different kinds of fish and birds?

Yes, God made the many different kinds of fish and birds.

Did God make many different animals on the earth?

Yes, God made many different animals on the earth.

Did God make the first man and woman on the earth?

Yes, God made the first man and woman on the earth, Adam and Eve.

The Angels

God's first creation was the Angels.
God created the Angels to share His happiness in Heaven.
God is so loving that He wants to share His happiness.
That is why He created Angels.
That is why He created us too.

The Song of the Angels

The Angels

God created the Angels first.
Angels are created spirits.
A spirit does not have a body.
Angels are invisible to us.

Angels have great knowledge.
Angels have great power.
Angels know things without
having to think about them.

You are very different from an
Angel.
You study and think about
things.
You have an invisible soul but
a visible body.
Your body and soul belong to
each other forever.
God created no one else like
you.

An Angel does not have a body
so you cannot see an Angel.
Angels have great knowledge
and power.
Angels always see and adore the Face of God.

Angels do many things for God.
Countless Angels praise God in Heaven.
Countless Angels are present at every Mass being offered in the
world.
The Angels adore God while we pray at Mass.

Queen of the Angels.

The Angels

Guardian Angels take care of us. Each human being in the world has a Guardian Angel. God gives each person an Angel to help him to be good.

God wants our Guardian Angel to help us get to Heaven. Our Guardian Angels help us always. My Guardian Angel keeps me out of danger.

My Guardian Angel reminds me to think of God. We should pray to our Guardian Angel every day. We like to say our Guardian Angel prayer every evening.

"Angel of God, my guardian dear To whom God's love entrusts me here."

Guardian Angels take care of us.

God loves me so much He gave me one of His Angels to protect me.

"Ever this day be at my side,
To light, to guard,
To rule, to guide. Amen."

My Guardian Angel will help me get to Heaven.

The Angels

Who made the Angels?

God made the Angels.

Why did God make Angels?

God made Angels to be happy with Him in Heaven.

What are Angels?

Angels are created spirits without bodies.

What do Angels do?

They love and adore God.

What are Guardian Angels?

God made Guardian Angels to be with us to protect us.

Does each person have a Guardian Angel?

Yes, each of us has our own Guardian Angel.

Will my Guardian Angel help me to get to Heaven?

Yes, my Guardian Angel will help me every day so I can get to Heaven.

God Our Creator

We know that God is the Creator of all things.

We also know that God created us.

God did not need to create us.

But He created you and me because He loves us.

He wants to share His happiness in Heaven with us.

God wants us to be in Heaven with Him forever.

God in Heaven

God Our Creator

God created us because He loves us.
He did not create us and then forget about us.
He sends each one of us a Guardian Angel to protect us.

God also keeps us in His mind all the time.
God keeps us in His heart all the time.
We think about our mother and our father often because we love them.

God thinks about us all the time because He loves us.
We should think about God often to show Him that we love Him.
We should think about God often because He loves us.

Adoration of the Trinity

God Our Creator

God made us because He loves us.
God wants us to go to Heaven to be with Him.
We want to go to Heaven when we die.

But we must be good to go to Heaven.
God gave us some rules to follow so that we can be good.
When we follow God's rules, we will be good.

If we are good, we can go to Heaven to be with God when we die.
Holy men have said that Heaven is very beautiful.
They have said that Heaven is wonderful.

St. Paul said that Heaven is wonderful.
He said our eyes and ears have not seen or heard anything so wonderful.
St. Paul said we cannot even imagine how beautiful Heaven is.

Heaven is so beautiful and wonderful because God is there.

Heaven is wonderful because God is there.

God Our Creator

Who made you?

God made me.

Why did God make you?

God made me to show His goodness and to make me happy with Him in Heaven forever.

What must you do to be happy with God in Heaven?

To be happy with God in Heaven, I must know Him, love Him, and serve Him in this world.

Who will help me to get to Heaven?

God will give me all the help I need to get to Heaven.

Will my Guardian Angel help me?

Yes, God has sent each one of us a Guardian Angel to help us.

What is Heaven?

Heaven is God's home. Holy people have said it is so wonderful and so beautiful, we cannot even imagine it.

Angels

Adam and Eve

God often visited Adam and Eve in the Garden.

God created our first parents.
God created a man named Adam, and a woman named Eve.
Adam and Eve were husband and wife.

God put Adam and Eve in a beautiful Garden.
This Garden was called the Garden of Paradise.
God wanted Adam and Eve to be very happy.

God planted this Garden with many fruit trees filled with delicious fruit.
God told Adam that he was in charge of all the animals.
Adam named all the animals God created.
Adam and Eve were very intelligent.

God often visited Adam and Eve in the Garden.
God gave Adam and Eve only one rule.
This was a rule for them to obey.
They were not to eat of the fruit of the
Tree of Knowledge of Good and Evil.
God wanted to test them.
Did they love Him enough to obey Him?

Adam and Eve

God gave Adam and Eve a rule to follow.
God's rule was this:

> **Do not eat of the tree in the middle of the Garden called the Tree of the Knowledge of Good and Evil.**

God warned them that if they disobeyed Him, they would die.
Adam and Eve obeyed God and continued to enjoy the Garden.
But one day, a visitor came to the Garden.
It was not God.
It was the devil.

The Garden

When God created the Angels, a few of the Angels rebelled against God.

They had a big fight with the good Angels.
So God sent the rebellious Angels to hell to be punished.

Since that time they have been called devils.
The leader of the devils is Satan.

Satan is ugly, evil, and a wicked liar.

All devils are really ugly, evil, and deceitful,
but they pretend to be beautiful and good.

One day, Satan pretended to be a talking serpent.
He spoke in soft words to Eve.

St. Michael

He told her the biggest lie.
The devil told Eve that if she ate the fruit
of the Tree of Knowledge of Good and Evil,
she would not die but she would become like God!

What a terrible lie!

We read in the Bible that Jesus called Satan "the father of lies."

Adam and Eve

The devil lied and told Eve she would not die
if she ate the fruit forbidden by God.

Eve looked at the fruit, and thought it might be good to eat.
Eve decided that disobeying God might be good for her.
The Holy Bible says that Eve "saw that the tree was good to eat,
and fair to the eyes, and delightful to behold."
Then Eve took the forbidden fruit, and ate it.

Eve wanted Adam to eat the forbidden fruit.
Then Eve gave Adam the forbidden fruit to eat.
Adam ate the forbidden fruit.
Adam and Eve disobeyed God Who created them.

Eve gave Adam the forbidden fruit to eat.

When someone disobeys God, it is called a sin.
Adam and Eve disobeyed God.
Adam and Eve committed the first sin on earth.
It is called Original Sin.
Adam and Eve were the first parents on earth.
So everyone else born after them inherits Original Sin on their souls.

Even though Adam and Eve sinned, God still loved them.
God said they would be punished for their sin, however.
They would get sick. They would have pain.
They would have to work for their food and clothes.
They would have to study. They would die someday.
Worst of all, God the Father closed the gates of Heaven.

But He made them a Big Promise.
God promised to send Adam and Eve and their children a Savior.
After the Savior came, God would open the gates of Heaven again.

Adam and Eve are forced to leave the Garden.

Adam and Eve

Who were the first man and woman created by God?

Our first parents, Adam and Eve, were the first man and woman created by God.

What is sin?

Sin is disobedience to God.

Who committed the first sin?

The bad Angels, called devils, committed the first sin.

Where did God put the devils?

God put the devils in hell, a place of eternal suffering and punishment.

Where are the good Angels?

The good Angels are in Heaven with God.

Who committed the first sin on earth?

Our first parents, Adam and Eve, committed the first sin on earth.

Is this sin passed on to us from Adam?

Yes, this sin is passed on to us from Adam.

What is this sin in us called?

This sin in us is called Original Sin.

Did God close the gates of Heaven?

Yes, after Original Sin, God closed the gates of Heaven.

What Promise did God make to Adam and Eve?

God promised to send Adam and Eve and their children a Savior Who would open the gates of Heaven.

The Ten Commandments

A long, long time ago, in a land far away called Egypt, a little Israelite boy was born. He was named Moses. Moses grew up to be a good and holy man because his mother taught him about God and taught him to be good.

One day, God appeared to Moses in a burning bush.

God told Moses: "I have seen the suffering of My People in Egypt. I will send you to Pharaoh that you may bring My People, the children of Israel, out of Egypt."

The Israelites were slaves to the Egyptians. So at first, the Pharaoh did not want to let them go. God told Moses that He would help Moses free the Israelites.

Moses and the Burning Bush

God sent many punishments to the Egyptians. They finally allowed Moses and the Israelites to leave Egypt.

During the journey, Moses went up on a high mountain where God appeared to him again. This time God told Moses that if the Israelites obeyed His Laws, they would be free from sin.

Sin is a worse slavery than the slavery the children of Israel suffered in Egypt. God gave the Israelites the Ten Commandments to help keep them free from sin, their worst enemy. God also promised that if the Israelites kept His Commandments, He would protect them from their enemies on earth.

The Ten Commandments

A long time ago, God appeared to Moses on a high mountain. Moses was the leader of the Israelites.

God told Moses that He would protect the children of Israel. But to receive God's special protection, they must obey Him.

God gave Moses ten rules or Ten Commandments. The Israelites were to be God's Chosen People. From the Israelites, the Savior would be born. God gave the Ten Commandments to His Chosen People. God wanted them to be holy, to help them not to sin.

God created us. He knows what makes us happy, and God also knows what makes us sad. God knows we are happy when we follow His Commandments. God knows we are very sad when we do not follow His Commandments.

We show God we love Him when we obey His Commandments.

Moses and the Ten Commandments

The Ten Commandments

God gave Moses the
Ten Commandments
for His Chosen People.

But God wants all of
us to follow His Ten
Commandments.
God wants all of us to be
happy.

God wants all of us to
go to Heaven.
God wanted to show us how
important are the
Ten Commandments.
So God wrote the Ten
Commandments on two
large pieces of stone.
They are often called
tablets of stone.

Moses and the Ten Commandments

On one tablet were
the first three
commandments.
The first three commandments are rules to adore God.
The other seven commandments are rules about our neighbor.

These Ten Commandments are rules to keep us from sin.
These Ten Commandments guide us so we will be happy on earth.
These Ten Commandments tell us what to do to get to Heaven.

The Ten Commandments

Who was Moses?

Moses was a holy man to whom God gave His Ten Commandments on stone.

To whom did God give the Ten Commandments?

God gave the Ten Commandments to the people of Israel through Moses.

What are the Ten Commandments?

The Ten Commandments are rules of God for all mankind.

Why should we obey the Ten Commandments?

We should obey the Ten Commandments because God, our Heavenly Father, gave them to us so that we would know what we must do to always be happy and please Him.

Besides believing in God, what else must I do to get to Heaven?

Besides believing in God, I must keep His Commandments.

Will we get to Heaven if we obey God's Ten Commandments?

Yes, we will go to Heaven if we obey God's Ten Commandments.

The First Commandment

The First Commandment of God is the most important.
That is why God made it the First Commandment.
The First Commandment is:

> **I am the Lord thy God;**
> **thou shalt not have strange gods before Me.**

The First Commandment has two parts.
In the first part, God is telling us that He is God.
He is telling us that He is the only God.
He is telling us that there is no other God.
He is telling us that no one else is God.
He Alone is our Lord and our God.

God loves us. God created us.
Because God created us, He knows how we can be happy.
God made rules for us to follow so we would be happy.

God is our Lord Who gives us rules to follow.
God is our Father Who loves us.
God is our loving Father Who created us.

Moses and the Golden Calf

The First Commandment

The First Commandment is:

**I am the Lord thy God;
thou shalt not have strange gods before Me.**

In the last lesson, we read about the first part of this Commandment.

Now we will learn about the second part of the First Commandment.
"Thou shalt not have strange gods before Me."
You shall have no strange gods before Me, God commands us.

God means that no one and no thing is more important than God.
We are not to make anyone or anything in our lives more important
than God.
Nothing is more important in our lives than God.

If we choose to play with our toys and not say our prayers when we
should, we are telling God our toys are more important than God.

If we choose to play with our friends and not go to Mass on Sunday,
we are putting our friends before God.

God the Father

The First Commandment

The First Commandment of God is:

> **I am the Lord thy God;
> thou shalt not have strange gods before Me.**

The First Commandment reminds us that we owe God everything.

God created us.
If God did not make us, we would not be.
God gave us our mother and our father.
God may have given us brothers and sisters.
God gave us our family.

All good things come from God.
God is all good and all holy.
We want to adore God because He is all good.
We want to worship God because He is all holy.

The First Commandment teaches us to adore God
and to worship God.
We must worship the one true God and Him alone.
We must believe in God.
We must love God.
We must pray to God.

The Last Judgment

We must love God above all things
because He is our loving Father and Creator.
We show our love for God when we obey His Commandments.

The First Commandment

What is the First Commandment of God?
The First Commandment of God is: I am the Lord thy God; thou shalt not have strange gods before Me.

What does the First Commandment command me to do?
The First Commandment commands me to love God, to adore God, and to pray to Him.

What does the First Commandment command me not to do?
The First Commandment tells me not to make anyone or anything more important than God.

How do we adore and worship God?
We adore and worship God by praying to Him, especially at Mass.

What does the First Commandment forbid me to do?
The First Commandment forbids me to neglect saying my daily prayers, or to purposely think of other things while I am praying.

The Golden Calf

The Second and Third Commandments

The Second Commandment of God is:

Thou shalt not take the name of the Lord thy God in vain.

God is commanding us to use His name in a respectful way.
God wants us to talk about Him with reverence.
God wants us to use His name in prayer.

When we say the holy name of Jesus, we bow our heads.
This reminds us that Jesus is God.
This reminds us that we should love and obey God, our Creator.
God is holy. God's name is holy, too.
When we say God's name in a loving way,
we are showing God that we love Him.

When we make the Sign of the Cross, we must make it in a loving way.
The Sign of the Cross gives honor to God the Father our Creator, God the Son our Savior, and God the Holy Spirit.

Jesus is God.

Always make the Sign of the Cross with love and respect.
"In the name of the Father, and of the Son, and of the Holy Spirit. Amen."
Saying the name of God in a careless way is taking God's holy name in vain.
We show our love for God when we obey His Commandments.

The Second and Third Commandments

The Second Commandment of God is:

Thou shalt not take the name of the Lord thy God in vain.

The apostles were special friends of Jesus.
When the apostles worked miracles,
they always used the Holy Name of Jesus.

They said to a crippled man,
"In the Name of Jesus, arise and walk."

The Holy Name of Jesus is so special
that some say it in a reverent prayer during the day.
They say, "Jesus, I love You."

Peter and John heal in the Holy Name of Jesus.

The name of Jesus is very powerful. We should say "Jesus" lovingly whenever we are tempted to do something bad.

Whenever we say the name of Jesus with devotion,
we give God great praise and glory.

Saying the name of Jesus is the shortest, the easiest,
and the most powerful of prayers.

"Jesus, I love You."

Jesus the Comforter

The Second and Third Commandments

The Third Commandment of God is:

Remember thou keep holy the Lord's day.

Sunday is the Lord's day. Sunday is a special holy day.
God commands us to make Sunday a special holy day.
The Catholic Church teaches us that the best way to keep Sunday holy is to go to Mass on Sunday.
The Catholic Church says that we owe God a special time of love and devotion at least once a week.
Every Sunday, we go to Mass to worship God.
God made every day, but Sunday is very holy and special to Him.

The Resurrection

When we go to Mass, we must be very good.
We must say our prayers in a very loving way.
We must not play around at Mass, or talk during Mass.
We should be a good example at Mass and show the younger children how to be good in church.
We show our love for God when we obey His Commandments.

Christians keep Sunday as the Lord's Day because God the Son, Jesus Christ, rose from the dead on the first Easter Sunday.

The Third Commandment forbids me to miss Mass on Sunday through my own fault. It forbids me to misbehave in church. It also says I should not be late for Sunday Mass.

Pray in a loving way.

The Second and Third Commandments

What is the Second Commandment of God?

The Second Commandment of God is: Thou shalt not take the name of the Lord thy God in vain.

What does the Second Commandment command me to do?

The Second Commandment commands me to honor the Holy Name of Jesus.

What does the Second Commandment forbid me to do?

The Second Commandment forbids me to use the Holy Name of God or Jesus in a careless or angry way.

What is the Third Commandment of God?

The Third Commandment of God is: Remember thou keep holy the Lord's day.

What does the Third Commandment command me to do?

The Third Commandment commands me to attend Mass on Sundays and Holy Days.

What does the Third Commandment forbid me to do?

The Third Commandment forbids me to miss Mass on Sundays or Holy Days through my own fault.

WEEK NINE: Day 1

First Quarter Review

Please review the Catechism questions and answers for Weeks One and Two. Ask your child to give you the Catechism answers as accurately as possible from memory.

WEEK NINE: Day 2

First Quarter Review

Please review the Catechism questions and answers for Weeks Three and Four. Ask your child to give you the Catechism answers as accurately as possible from memory.

WEEK NINE: Day 3

First Quarter Review

Please review the Catechism questions and answers for Weeks Five and Six. Ask your child to give you the Catechism answers as accurately as possible from memory.

WEEK NINE: Day 4

First Quarter Review

Please review the Catechism questions and answers for Weeks Seven and Eight. Ask your child to give you the Catechism answers as accurately as possible from memory.

The Last Supper

The Fourth Commandment

The Fourth Commandment of God is:

Honor thy father and thy mother.

Before everyone else on this earth, we must love our parents most of all because they gave us life.

We must respect our parents.

We must obey our parents.

Jesus honored Mary and Joseph.

God gave me my parents to love me and to take care of me.
My parents teach me about God.
My parents teach me about the Catholic Faith.
My parents give me a house to live in.
My parents provide me with food and clothes.

I need to be very good to my parents, as Jesus was to His parents.
I obey Jesus when I obey His Commandments.
I obey Jesus when I obey my parents.

When we read about the saints, we learn that
they obeyed their parents.
God is pleased when we obey our parents.
We show our love for God when we obey His Commandments.

I need to be very good to my parents, as Jesus was to His parents.

The Fourth Commandment

The Fourth Commandment of God is:

Honor thy father and thy mother.

The first three Commandments of God
command us how to worship God.
We are commanded to honor our parents after God.

In this world, no one on earth is as important as our parents.
Parents love their children with a special deep love.
No one loves us the way our mother
and our father love us.

Children must have a special love
for their parents.
We must obey our parents in a
loving way.
We must be kind to our parents.
We should think of doing good
things for our parents even when
we are not asked.

Jesus does chores.

We must do some chores around
the house to help mother and
father.
Sometimes children help take out
the trash.
Sometimes children clean up
something spilled.
Children can help teach a little
brother or sister.
Children can play with a little
brother or sister when mother is busy.

The Fourth Commandment

The Fourth Commandment of God is:

Honor thy father and thy mother.

When Jesus lived on earth,
He always obeyed His mother Mary and His foster father Joseph.
When Jesus was a Boy on earth,
He listened to the words of Mary and Joseph.

Joseph taught Him about being a carpenter.
Even though Jesus is God, He obeyed Joseph.
Jesus learned to use the carpenter's tools,
and learned to make the things Joseph taught Him.
Joseph taught Jesus to be a good carpenter,
to do the best work He could.
Jesus was always obedient to Joseph.

Jesus helped Mary when she cooked the meals.
Jesus helped Mary to keep their home clean.
Jesus went with Mary and Joseph to pray
to His Father in Heaven.
Jesus always did what He could to please His parents.

God wants us to be good to our parents.
God wants us to be obedient to our parents.
God is happy when we are obedient and kind to our parents.

God wants us to honor our parents.
We honor God when we honor our parents.
We show our love for God when we obey His Commandments.

The Fourth Commandment

What is the Fourth Commandment of God?

The Fourth Commandment is: Honor thy father and thy mother.

What does the Fourth Commandment of God command me to do?

The Fourth Commandment of God commands me to love, honor, and obey my parents.

What does the Fourth Commandment forbid me to do?

The Fourth Commandment forbids me to disobey my parents. It forbids me to talk back to my parents, or to be mean to them.

The Holy Family

Did Jesus always obey His parents?

Yes, Jesus always obeyed His parents.

Must we obey our parents when it is very hard?

Yes, we must obey our parents even when it is very hard.

Must we obey our parents when they teach us?

Yes, we must obey our parents when they teach us, especially when they teach us our religion.

Jesus always obeyed His parents.

The Fifth and Sixth Commandments

The Fifth Commandment of God is:

Thou shalt not kill.

God is the Creator; He gave us life.
We may not take the life of a human being unjustly.
We may not hurt others in anger.
God is our Father in Heaven.
God is a loving Father.
When we play with our brothers and sisters,
we must not hurt them.
When we play with our friends, we must not hurt them.
We must not get angry over the wrong things.
We must not fight just because we feel like it.
We must not get angry or hurt anyone because we feel nasty.
We must not argue just because we feel like being mean.
We should try to be good to everyone we meet.

Jesus told us:

**This is My Commandment:
that you love one another as I have loved you.**

Long ago, the non-Christians said about the Christians:
"See how they love one another."
If we want to obey God, we must love one another as God loves us.

The Fifth and Sixth Commandments

The Fifth Commandment of God is:

Thou shalt not kill.

This commandment means that we must not commit murder.

We must be careful not to hurt our neighbors and friends.
Sometimes children throw things
and they accidentally hurt someone.
If we hurt someone because we have been careless,
then we are breaking the Fifth Commandment.
We must be careful when we play.
We may not play in such a careless way that someone gets hurt.

The Fifth Commandment also commands us to take proper
care of our own bodily health. We must not make ourselves
sick by eating only junk food and sweets. We are not allowed
to mistreat our bodies.
We must not ride our bikes where it is not safe.
We must not skate where it is not safe.
We must make sure the car doors are locked when we go for a ride in
the car. We should use our seat belts.

The Fifth Commandment commands us to take care of our own health
and that of our neighbor.
We show our love for God when we obey His Commandments.

The Fifth and Sixth Commandments

The Sixth Commandment of God is:

Thou shalt not commit adultery.

Adultery is a sin that children cannot commit.
But children need to remember to be pure and modest.

When we are baptized, our souls are filled with Supernatural Grace.
Baptism makes our souls strong in the love of God.
A newly baptized soul is very pure and strong in Supernatural Grace.

The Holy Family and St. John the Baptist

The Sixth Commandment commands us to keep our
souls and bodies strong in virtue by being pure and modest.

We must not go to bad movies or look at bad pictures.
We must keep our minds and hearts and bodies pure and modest.

We must not say bad words or listen to bad words.
We must not watch bad television shows.

God loves boys and girls.
God loves modest boys and girls.
If we hear bad words, or see bad movies or television shows,
we should say some prayers and walk away.
We can say a Hail Mary.
God wants us to be pure and modest in what we say,
in what we do, and in what we think.
We show our love for God when we obey His Commandments.

God loves modest boys and girls.

The Fifth and Sixth Commandments

What is the Fifth Commandment of God?

The Fifth Commandment of God is: Thou shalt not kill.

What does the Fifth Commandment of God command me to do?

The Fifth Commandment of God commands me to take proper care of my health and the health of others.

What does the Fifth Commandment of God forbid me to do?

The Fifth Commandment of God forbids me to murder anyone, or to hurt myself. It also forbids me to hurt anyone. It forbids me to be careless about my own health or the health of my neighbor.

Cain killed Abel.

What is the Sixth Commandment of God?

The Sixth Commandment of God is: Thou shalt not commit adultery.

What does the Sixth Commandment command me to do?

The Sixth Commandment commands me to be pure in what I think, and say, and do.

What does the Sixth Commandment forbid?

The Sixth Commandment forbids me to say bad words or to listen to bad words. It forbids me to look at bad pictures, bad movies, or bad television shows.

What should I do if I am near bad pictures, bad movies, or bad television shows?

If I am near bad pictures, movies, or television shows, I should quickly say a Hail Mary and go away or turn the TV off.

Jesus and Mary

49

The Seventh Commandment

The Seventh Commandment of God is:

Thou shalt not steal.

It is against the Commandment of God to take something
that does not belong to us without permission.
To steal means to take as our own things that are not ours.

We may not take things that belong to our parents.
We may not take things that belong to our brothers and sisters.
We may not take things that belong to our friends.

The Tribute Money

God wants me to have some things.
But I may not take things that belong to someone else.
And others may not take things that belong to me.

Taking things that belong to someone else is stealing.
Older people go to jail for stealing.

If I borrow something, I must return it.
If I borrow a book from the library, I must return it.
If I find something, I should try to return it to the owner.

We must give back anything we take.
God wants us to be happy with the things we have.
We show our love for God when we obey His Commandments.

The Unfaithful Servant

The Seventh Commandment

The Seventh Commandment of God is:

Thou shalt not steal.

God is commanding us not to take what belongs to someone else. We must not steal the things that belong to someone else.

We must be truthful. We are truthful when we do not take things that belong to someone else. For instance, we must not cheat when we take our tests. If we steal the correct answers from the answer key, we are being dishonest. We have stolen the answers we are not supposed to have.

If we steal a piece of candy from the store, we are committing a sin against the Seventh Commandment. If we steal money from mother's purse, we are committing a sin against the Seventh Commandment. If we steal a toy from someone, we are committing a sin against the Seventh Commandment.

Jesus loves children.

We offend God when we steal. We must give back what we have stolen, and ask God's forgiveness. Then God will forgive us.

The Seventh Commandment

The Seventh Commandment of God is:

Thou shalt not steal.

Sometimes people are not happy with what God has given them.
And they take things from other people.

Sometimes children take other children's baseballs or games,
and never give them back. That is stealing.
Sometimes children take other children's candy. That is stealing.

If you destroy someone's property
and do not pay for it or fix it, that is stealing.
If you deliberately ride your bike over the flower bushes of the
lady next door, you are stealing her flowers
unless you pay for the flower bushes.
If you borrow your friend's toy, and break it,
you are stealing unless you fix it or buy your friend a new toy.

If you are using your friend's toy, and it breaks accidentally when
you are playing with it, you should tell your friend and try to find
a way to repair it or pay for it.
You must always be very careful when you use
or borrow anyone else's property.

Stealing is taking what belongs to someone else
without their permission.
Stealing is also destroying what belongs to another.
If you take or destroy what belongs to another,
you must return it or pay for it or buy another one.

The Seventh Commandment

What is the Seventh Commandment of God?

The Seventh Commandment of God is: Thou shalt not steal.

What does the Seventh Commandment command us to do?

The Seventh Commandment commands us to respect things which belong to another.

What does the Seventh Commandment forbid us to do?

The Seventh Commandment forbids us to take or to destroy what belongs to another.

What must we do if we steal or destroy something?

If we steal something, we must return it.
If we destroy something, we must pay for it.

"Don't wake up Baby Jesus."

The Eighth Commandment

The Eighth Commandment of God is:

> **Thou shalt not bear false witness against thy neighbor.**

This means that we cannot tell an untrue story about someone.
God does not want us to say something false about our neighbor.
We must always tell the truth. When we do not tell the truth, we lie.
God teaches us that it is a sin to tell a lie.
If we tell a lie, we are disobeying God's Commandment.

We need to ask God to help us to always tell the truth.
Sometimes, when we know we will be punished,
it is hard to tell the truth.
But telling lies is much worse than the punishment.
If we do not admit that we broke something, and our little brother is
punished instead, then we have committed two sins instead of one.
We have been unjust to our little brother.
It is very difficult to have a happy family if
someone lies.
No one knows what is really true or
untrue.

The devil in hell is called the Father of
Lies.
The devil lied and told Eve
that disobeying God would make her like
God.
But God is Truth. God is Good.
We want to tell the truth.
We want to be like Jesus.
We do not want to be a liar – like the devil.
We show our love for God when we obey
His Commandments.

St. Andrew

The Eighth Commandment

The Eighth Commandment of God is:

Thou shalt not bear false witness against thy neighbor.

St. Peter Denies Jesus

The Eighth Commandment commands us not to lie.

We must tell the truth about ourselves.

We must tell the truth about our neighbors.

We should not talk about the faults of our neighbors.

For instance, if someone has a fault or a bad habit, it is not our business to tell other children,

but sometimes it is important to tell our parents.

We must never tell a lie.
George Washington, our first American president, became famous as a boy because he would not tell a lie to his parents.

Long ago, the pagans wanted to kill the Christians.
But Christians would not lie.
They told the truth about their love for Jesus Christ.
They said they were Christians even though they knew they would be killed.

Jesus wants us to be good and tell the truth.
Jesus wants us to use our words to tell the truth.
Jesus said, "Love your neighbor as yourself."
He meant that we must do what is good for our neighbor.

Christians told the truth about Jesus.

The Eighth Commandment

The Eighth Commandment of God is:

Thou shalt not bear false witness against thy neighbor.

The Eighth Commandment commands us to be truthful.
The Eighth Commandment commands us not to lie.

When we tell the truth, we please God very much.
We displease God and hurt our neighbor when we tell a lie.
Sometimes we want to blame someone else for our own mistakes.
But that is wrong.
We must always tell the truth.

Jesus always tells the truth.
Jesus said, "I am the Truth."
No one can be more truthful than Jesus.
We want to be good, and be like Jesus as much as we can be.
So we want to tell the truth.

God made us.
He knows that if we tell the truth, we will be happy.
God knows that if we tell lies, we will be very unhappy.

Someday, we want to be happy with God in Heaven.

Jesus said, "I am the Truth."

To be happy with God in Heaven, we must keep His Commandments.
To be happy with God in Heaven, we must always tell the truth.
We show our love for God when we obey His Commandments.

The Eighth Commandment

What is the Eighth Commandment of God?

The Eighth Commandment of God is: Thou shalt not bear false witness against thy neighbor.

What does the Eighth Commandment command us to do?

The Eighth Commandment commands us to tell the truth at all times, and to speak well of our neighbor.

What does the Eighth Commandment forbid?

The Eighth Commandment forbids telling lies. It especially forbids telling lies about our family and our neighbors.

We should act like the Holy Family.

The Ninth and Tenth Commandments

The Ninth Commandment of God is:

Thou shalt not covet thy neighbor's wife.

The Ninth Commandment is not for children.

The Ninth Commandment commands adults
not to want to marry someone else's wife or husband.

It is important to pray for all; people need God's help to be good.

We show our love for God when we obey His Commandments.

The Marriage of Mary and Joseph

The Ninth and Tenth Commandments

The Tenth Commandment of God is:

Thou shalt not covet thy neighbor's goods.

God is telling us that we should not covet, or seriously desire,
the property of our neighbor. God is telling us that if we covet,
or deeply desire, someone's property,
we are going against His Commandment.

We should want good things,
but we must want them in the right way.
We must want them in such a good way that we
work for them honestly.

Suppose you see a beautiful new blue bike.
You see the new bike on the sidewalk.
You really do want that beautiful blue bike very much.
You want it so much you think of little else.
You talk of little else.
You want that bike every time you see someone with it.
You do nothing to earn it or buy it,
and you would be willing to do something wrong to get it.

If we "covet" something, we want it very much in the wrong way.
That deep desire to want someone else's goods is a sin.
It is a sin against the Tenth Commandment.
Jesus commands us to be happy with what we have.

The Ninth and Tenth Commandments

The Tenth Commandment of God is:

Thou shalt not covet thy neighbor's goods.

God commands us by this Commandment that we must not seriously desire to take what belongs to our neighbor.
God is very unhappy when anyone desires to steal.

God is so unhappy with anyone who steals from anyone, that He has made two Commandments about stealing.
The Seventh Commandment is:
Thou shalt not steal.
The Tenth Commandment commands us that we should not even seriously desire to steal.

God has made two Commandments against stealing: the seventh and tenth Commandments.

When someone steals, he must return what he stole and ask God for forgiveness by going to Confession.

Jesus in Glory

Someone who covets what another person has must ask God for forgiveness in Confession.

The Ninth and Tenth Commandments

What is the Ninth Commandment of God?

The Ninth Commandment of God is: Thou shalt not covet thy neighbor's wife.

What is the Tenth Commandment of God?

The Tenth Commandment of God is: Thou shalt not covet thy neighbor's goods.

What does the Tenth Commandment command me to do?

The Tenth Commandment commands me to respect the property of my neighbor. It also commands me to be happy with what I have.

What does the Tenth Commandment forbid?

The Tenth Commandment forbids having a deep desire to steal another's property.

Jesus washes the apostles' feet.

The Coming of Our Savior Jesus Christ

When Adam and Eve were disobedient to God in the Garden of Paradise, God the Father closed the gates of Heaven to them and all their children.
But God the Father promised He would not leave them.
God promised to send a Savior to open the gates of Heaven again.

God gave Moses the Ten Commandments to help the people to be good before the Savior came.

Finally, God sent His Son, Jesus Christ, to be the promised Savior.

Jesus Christ is the second Person of the Blessed Trinity.
Jesus is the Son of God.
Jesus is God.

Adam and Eve are sent from the Garden.

The Coming of
Our Savior Jesus Christ

Jesus said: "The Father and I are One."
God the Father sent His only Son, Jesus Christ, to be the Savior.
Jesus came into this world to save us from sin.
Jesus came into this world to save us from hell.
Jesus came into this world to open the gates of Heaven for us.

Jesus came into this world to save us from sin.

The Coming of Our Savior Jesus Christ

We know that Jesus Christ is the Son of God.
God the Father sent the Angel Gabriel to Mary.
Mary was very holy. She did not have any sin at all.

The Angel Gabriel said to Mary: "Hail, Mary, full of Grace. The Lord is with you. Blessed are you among women."

"Full of Grace" means that Mary was filled with holiness.
The Blessed Virgin Mary had no sin.

The Angel Gabriel said to Mary: "Hail Mary, full of Grace."

Then the Angel Gabriel told Mary that God had chosen her to be the Mother of Jesus, His only Son.
Mary said: "I am the handmaid of God.
Let it be done to me according to the word of God."

Mary was happy to do God's Will. Mary was happy to be the Mother of Jesus, the Son of God. She went to visit her cousin Elizabeth who also was going to have a baby. God gave St. Elizabeth a special Grace. When Elizabeth heard Mary greet her, she felt her own baby's joy and reverence for God.

Elizabeth knew that Mary was to be the Mother of God. Elizabeth knelt down in front of Mary and said, "How is it that the Mother of my God should come to visit me?" Mary said, "My soul magnifies the Lord, for God has done great things for me."

Mary went to visit Elizabeth, her cousin.

The Coming of Our Savior Jesus Christ

God the Father wanted to choose a holy man to be the foster father of Jesus. Saint Joseph was a very holy man. He was a very good man. We often call him "Good Saint Joseph."

God loved Saint Joseph very, very much. God told Saint Joseph to take Mary as his wife.

After Mary and Joseph were married, they went to Bethlehem. It was in Bethlehem that Jesus was born. Since there was no room at the inn, they stayed in a stable.

Jesus was born in a stable.

Jesus was born in a stable in Bethlehem.
He was born on the first Christmas Day.
Jesus was surrounded by the Angels.
Some of the Angels appeared to the shepherds in Bethlehem.
They told the shepherds about Jesus.
These shepherds came to visit Him in the stable.
They adored Jesus, the little King of Kings.

Jesus Christ, the Son of God, came to us as a little Baby.
God the Father is the Father of Jesus.
Saint Joseph was the foster father of Jesus on earth.
Jesus is true God.
Jesus is true Man.

Jesus is God and Man.
Jesus is the Son of God.
Jesus is the Son of Mary.

The Shepherds Adore Jesus

The Coming of Our Savior Jesus Christ

Did God become man?

Yes, the Second Person of the Blessed Trinity, the Son of God, became man.

What is the name of the Son of God made man?

The name of the Son of God made man is Jesus Christ.

When was Jesus born?

Jesus was born on the first Christmas Day, over 2000 years ago.

Who is the mother of Jesus?

The mother of Jesus is the Blessed Virgin Mary.

Who is the Father of Jesus?

The Father of Jesus is God the Father.

Who is Saint Joseph?

Saint Joseph is the foster father, that is, the guardian of Jesus on earth.

Jesus and Mary

Is Jesus Christ both God and man?

Yes, Jesus Christ is both God and man.

Why did the Son of God become man?

The Son of God became man to save us from our sins and to open the gates of Heaven for us.

The Holy Family: Jesus, Mary, and Joseph

Jesus Christ is the Son of God, the second Person of the Holy Trinity.
Jesus could have just appeared on earth.
He could have come as a full-grown man.
But Jesus Christ wanted to teach us something important.

Jesus wanted to teach us that a family is very important.
So Jesus came to earth as a little Baby in a family.

God the Father chose the Blessed Virgin Mary to be the Mother of Jesus. God the Father chose Saint Joseph to be the foster father of Jesus on earth.

Jesus loved being with His family.

We call Jesus' family "The Holy Family."

We should pray to Jesus, Mary, and Joseph.

The Holy Family will help make our own family holy and pleasing to God.

The Holy Family with St. John and Elizabeth

The Holy Family:
Jesus, Mary, and Joseph

When Jesus was still a little Baby,
there were three kings who were very well educated.
They were called the Three Wise Men from the east.
They read the Bible and other holy books.
They knew that it was time for the Savior to be born.
They knew a special star in the sky would
lead the way to the Savior.
The three wise kings traveled far.
They followed the special star to the city of Jerusalem.
When they arrived in the city, they went to see the king
of Jerusalem. They asked King Herod if he knew where the King
was to be born.

The three wise kings traveled far.

The Three Wise Men said they wanted to adore the Infant King.
This made Herod angry.
Then Herod told a big lie.
Herod said that he also would like to go and adore the child.
He told the three kings to come back and tell him where they found
the Infant King.

The Three Wise Men followed the star to Bethlehem
and found the Baby Jesus.
The Holy Bible tells us the story.
"Entering into the house, they found the Child with Mary,
His mother, and falling down, they adored Him.
"And opening their treasures, they offered Him gifts:
gold, frankincense, and myrrh."
Mary and Joseph were very happy.

The Wise Men adore the Baby Jesus.

The Holy Family:
Jesus, Mary, and Joseph

The Holy Family was very happy.
They were together all the time.
Saint Joseph took care of Mary and Jesus.

One night, an Angel came to Saint Joseph from God the Father.
The Holy Bible tells the story.
"An Angel of the Lord appeared in sleep to Joseph, saying:
Arise, and take the Child and His mother, and flee into Egypt.
Stay there until I command you to return.
Because King Herod will seek the Child to kill Him."
Saint Joseph immediately arose from his bed. He took the Child
Jesus and His mother Mary, and quickly departed into a neighboring
country called Egypt.

The Holy Family in Egypt

Herod was "exceedingly" jealous. He was afraid the new King would take over his kingdom! He ordered his soldiers to kill all the boy babies in Bethlehem.

The Holy Family stayed safely in Egypt until Herod died. Then one night, an Angel of the Lord appeared again to Joseph. The Angel said: "Arise and take the Child and His mother, and go back to the land of Israel. For they are dead who sought the life of the Child." Joseph arose and took the Child Jesus and His mother Mary, and returned to the land of Israel. The Angel also told Saint Joseph to take the Holy Family to live in the town of Nazareth.

The Holy Family stayed safely in Egypt until Herod died.

The Holy Family:
Jesus, Mary, and Joseph

Did the Son of God come to this world as a Baby?
Yes, the Son of God came to this world as a Baby.

Who is the mother of Jesus?
The mother of Jesus is the Blessed Virgin Mary.

Who is the Father of Jesus?
The Father of Jesus is God the Father.

Who was the foster father of Jesus when He was on earth?
Saint Joseph was the foster father of Jesus on earth.

What do we call the three kings who visited Baby Jesus?
We call the three kings who visited Baby Jesus the Three Wise Men.

What was the name of the bad king?
King Herod was the bad king.

What did the bad king do?
King Herod killed all the baby boys who lived in Bethlehem.

Did an Angel appear to Saint Joseph?
Yes, an Angel appeared to Saint Joseph, the head of the Holy Family.

Into which country did the Holy Family flee to escape Herod?
The Holy Family fled into Egypt to escape Herod.

What is the name of the town where the Holy Family lived?
The Holy Family lived in Nazareth.

Jesus Grows Up

When Jesus was still a Baby, His parents took Him to the Temple. The Temple was another name for a church. It was the religious practice for parents to take their babies to the Temple. They would pray in the Temple. At the Temple, they would receive a special blessing. They would present the child to God. This was called the Presentation.

When Saint Joseph and the Blessed Virgin Mary took Jesus to the Temple, they met two special friends of God. The first person they met was Simeon. He was a holy man who spent much time in the Temple praying. God loved Simeon. God wanted to reward Simeon because he was a good and holy man. Simeon had asked God that he would not die until he had seen the Savior God promised Adam.

God was pleased with Simeon's prayer. God led Simeon into the Temple on the morning when the Holy Family came to present the Baby Jesus to God in the Temple. Joseph and Mary brought in the Baby Jesus. They gave the Baby to Simeon to hold. The Bible says Simeon "took Him into his arms."

Then Simeon said: "Now dismiss me, O Lord, because my eyes have seen Your salvation which you have prepared before the face of all peoples."

The second person Mary and Joseph met in the Temple was Anna. Anna was very old, probably ninety years old.
Anna was a holy lady who spent every day in the Temple.
She prayed and fasted "night and day," the Bible says.
Anna was allowed by God to recognize that Jesus is the Savior.
Anna told Joseph and Mary that she knew Jesus is the Savior.

The Presentation

Jesus Grows Up

The Holy Family lived very quietly in Nazareth.
St. Joseph was a carpenter.
Jesus helped His foster father in the carpenter shop.
Jesus helped His Mother around the house.

The neighbors marveled because Jesus was strong
and full of holy wisdom.

When Jesus was twelve years old, Joseph and Mary took
Jesus to the Temple in Jerusalem.

Jesus helped His foster father in the carpenter shop.

When it was time to go home, Joseph thought Jesus was with Mary and the other mothers. Mary thought Jesus was with Joseph and the other fathers.

After traveling for a day, they discovered that Jesus was still back in Jerusalem.

They quickly rushed back to Jerusalem. Mary and Joseph searched among their friends and relatives.
But they could not find Jesus.
For three days they searched for Jesus. They knew that Jesus is the Son of God, but they did not understand why Jesus had left them.

Mary and Joseph rushed back to Jerusalem.

Jesus Grows Up

When His mother Mary and foster father St. Joseph
did not find Jesus among their friends and relatives,
they returned to look for Him in the Temple in Jerusalem.
Mary and Joseph entered the Temple and found Jesus.
Jesus was sitting among the priests and teachers.
Mary and Joseph listened to Jesus.
Jesus was talking to the priests and the teachers.

Jesus was talking to the priests and the teachers.

Jesus was helping them to understand important things about God.
He was teaching them about God the Father.
The priests and teachers asked Him questions.

They were amazed.
How could this young Boy of twelve know so much about God?

Jesus talked about God's promise made to Adam. He talked about
God the Father sending a Savior.
The Bible says,
"All that heard Him were astonished at His wisdom and His answers."

Jesus told Mary and Joseph that He had remained in the Temple
to do the Will of God His Father in Heaven.
Jesus then went home with His mother Mary
and His foster father Saint Joseph.
The Holy Family returned to Nazareth.
The Holy Family lived in Nazareth for many years.
Jesus grew up in Nazareth.

"All that heard Him were astonished at His wisdom and His answers."

Jesus Grows Up

What was the Presentation?

Saint Joseph and the Blessed Virgin Mary presented the Baby Jesus to God the Father in the Temple in Jerusalem. This is called the Presentation.

Who was the holy man the Holy Family met in the Temple?

The holy man in the Temple was Simeon.

Who was the holy woman the Holy Family met in the Temple?

The holy woman in the Temple was Anna.

Where did the Holy Family go every year?

Every year, the Holy Family went to the Temple in Jerusalem to pray.

How many days did Joseph and Mary search for Jesus?

Joseph and Mary searched for Jesus for three days.

Where did Joseph and Mary find Jesus?

Joseph and Mary found Jesus in the Temple.

Who was Jesus talking to in the Temple?

Jesus was teaching the priests and teachers in the Temple.

Where did the Holy Family live?

The Holy Family lived in Nazareth.

WEEK EIGHTEEN: Day 1

Please review the Catechism and Catechism questions and answers for weeks 1 - 8. Ask your child to give you the Catechism answers as accurately as possible from memory.

WEEK EIGHTEEN: Day 2

Please review the Catechism and the Catechism questions and answers for weeks 9 - 12.
Ask your child to give you the Catechism answers as accurately as possible from memory.

WEEK EIGHTEEN: Day 3

Please review the Catechism and the Catechism questions and answers for weeks 13 - 15.
Ask your child to give you the Catechism answers as accurately as possible from memory.

WEEK EIGHTEEN: Day 4

Please review the Catechism and the Catechism questions and answers for weeks 16 - 17.
Ask your child to give you the Catechism answers as accurately as possible from memory.

The Presentation

Jesus and His Miracles

Jesus worked miracles to show us that He is God.
A miracle is something that is not according to
the usual things that happen.
A miracle is beyond the power of all people.
A miracle can be produced only by the power of God.
Jesus worked many miracles to prove to us that He is God.
The miracles of Jesus show how much God loves us.
God loves us and cares about us all the time.

Jesus Healing Jairus' Daughter

One time many people heard that Jesus was in the desert praying. They left their cities and towns to see and hear Jesus. The distance was so far and the crowds stayed so long, that everyone ran out of food and became very hungry. There were more than five thousand men, not counting all the women and children. Jesus felt sorry for them. He told them to sit down on the grass.

St. Matthew reported this event in his Gospel in the Bible: The apostles told Jesus they had only five loaves of bread and two fishes. Jesus said: "Bring them to Me." Then Jesus "took the five loaves and two fishes and looking up to heaven, He blessed, broke, and gave the loaves to His disciples." Then the disciples gave the food to all those who wanted to eat. Everyone ate, and they were filled!

And when the disciples took up what remained, they filled twelve baskets. "The number of those who ate was 5,000 men, besides women and children."

This is called the miracle of the loaves and fishes.
Jesus wanted to show through this miracle that He is God.
This miracle shows us God's power and His love and concern for us.

Multiplication of the Loaves and the Fishes

Jesus and His Miracles

Jesus loves us all so much that He worked many miracles for those who lived during His life on earth. When the Bible is read at Mass, we too can hear and learn about these holy events.

One time Jesus was speaking in someone's house. It was very crowded. It was so crowded, no one else could get in. There was a man who was very sick. He could not walk. His friends brought him to see Jesus on a stretcher. But they could not enter the house because it was so crowded. His friends climbed up on the roof, and cut a big hole in the roof. With great difficulty, they lifted the sick man on the stretcher up to the roof. Then they lowered him down through the hole in the roof.

Jesus was talking when suddenly coming down from the roof was the sick man on a stretcher. When Jesus saw how much Faith this man's friends had, He said to the sick man on the stretcher, "Be of good heart, Son, thy sins are forgiven thee."

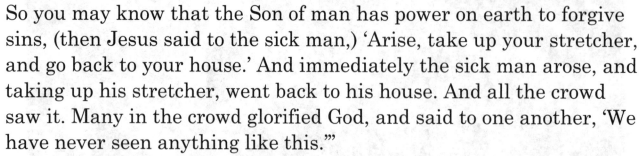

Many were surprised. They thought Jesus was going to cure the man of his illness. They knew that only God can forgive sins. Many still did not believe that Jesus was God.

Then Jesus said, "Which is easier to say, thy sins are forgiven, or arise and walk? So you may know that the Son of man has power on earth to forgive sins, (then Jesus said to the sick man,) 'Arise, take up your stretcher, and go back to your house.' And immediately the sick man arose, and taking up his stretcher, went back to his house. And all the crowd saw it. Many in the crowd glorified God, and said to one another, 'We have never seen anything like this.'"

Jesus showed that He loves us, and that He cares about us when we are sick. But most important, Jesus showed that as God, He can forgive our sins when our souls have become sick and weak with sin.

Jesus and His Miracles

Jesus loves us all so much that He is always ready to help us.
One day, Jesus was walking along the road with His friends.
They had to stop in the road because a large crowd was crossing.

It was a funeral procession.
A young boy had died.
His mother, a widow, was now tearfully following her friends
who were carrying the casket of her young dead son.
He was the only son of his mother.
Jesus saw the widow mother crying.
He knew that she was very, very sad.

She had lost her husband, and now she had lost her son.
When Jesus saw her, He was moved with pity
and mercy toward her.
He walked over to her in the road and said: "Do not weep."
Then He walked to the casket, and touched it.
He told the men carrying the casket to stand still.

Then He said in a loud voice: "Young man, I say to you, arise!"
And the young boy who was dead in the casket, sat up.
And he began to speak.
And Jesus lifted the boy out of the casket
and gave him to his mother.
Those in the procession and those following Jesus
began to glorify God.
"God has visited His people!" they said.

The news of this miracle spread
throughout all the country.
Jesus showed us all by His miracles that He is God.
Jesus also showed that He cares about families.

Jesus and His Miracles

Jesus worked many miracles, not only to prove that He is God, but also to show us how much He loves us. Jesus likes to show us how important the family is.

One time, there were two sisters, Martha and Mary. They had a brother named Lazarus. Jesus often visited Martha, Mary, and Lazarus in their home. The Bible says that Jesus loved Martha and her sister Mary, and Lazarus. They and their friends would listen to Jesus for hours when He taught them about God.

One day, while Jesus was in another town, Lazarus suddenly became very sick and died. Since He is God, Jesus knew that Lazarus had died.

Jesus often visited Martha, Mary, and Lazarus in their home.

Later, Jesus walked to the home of Martha and Mary. When He arrived, Lazarus had been already in the tomb for four days.

As Jesus was walking toward the house, Martha ran out to meet Him. Martha believed Jesus is God. Weeping, she said to Him, "Lord, if You had been here, my brother would not have died." She said, "You are Christ, the Son of the Living God Who has come into this world."

Then Mary, and many of their friends who had been visiting, came out to meet Jesus. When Jesus saw Martha and Mary weeping because Lazarus was dead, Jesus began to weep also. The friends said, "Look how much He loved him."

Jesus asked that they take Him to the tomb where Lazarus was buried. They went to the tomb which was a cave with a heavy stone sealing the opening. Jesus then said, "Take away the stone." The friends of Martha and Mary pushed the heavy stone. They finally moved the stone away from the opening to the tomb.

They moved the stone from the opening to the tomb.

Jesus and His Miracles

Jesus, lifting His eyes up to Heaven, said:
"My Father in Heaven, I give You thanks.
Because of those here who stand around,
that they may believe that You have sent Me."

And when He had said these things,
He cried with a loud voice: "Lazarus, come forth!"

At first, there was amazed silence. Then, suddenly, Lazarus who "had been dead came forth, bound feet and hands with winding bands" of cloths which had been wrapped around his dead body. His face was still covered with a cloth which had been put on him by his sisters. Jesus said, "Loose him, and let him go."

Jesus said, "Loose him, and let him go."

The large crowd stood in stunned silence. Then they began to praise and glorify God. Many knelt down and worshiped Jesus. Many who lived in that area saw the miracle of the raising of Lazarus from the dead. And they believed in Jesus. Several of the men suddenly began to run toward the town of Bethany, and other nearby towns, telling everyone what they had seen. Jesus had raised Lazarus from the dead!

Even the chief priests of the area said, "This Man does many miracles." Jesus was being talked about all over the country and even outside the country.

Besides raising from the dead Lazarus and the son of the widowed mother, Jesus also raised a young girl from the dead, the daughter of a soldier. Jesus cured many who were ill, especially those who could not hear or speak. He cured many who were sick with terrible diseases. He gave sight to many born blind. Many loved Jesus and He showed them how much God our Father in Heaven loves them.

Jesus cured many who were ill.

Jesus and His Teachings

God the Father sent His beloved Son,
Jesus Christ, into this world.
God had made a promise to Adam and Eve
that He would send a Savior.
When Jesus our Savior came,
He came as a Baby and grew up in the Holy Family.
When Jesus was thirty years old, He left Nazareth.
He began to teach about God His Father in Heaven
to people in the cities around the countryside.

Sermon on the Mount

The main teaching of Jesus Christ is that He is God made Man.
Jesus worked many miracles to prove that He is God.
He also worked miracles to show us that God loves us very much.
Jesus also wanted to teach us how happy we can be
if we love and obey Him.

Jesus taught that we must obey the Ten Commandments
which God the Father had given to Moses.
Jesus teaches us that we need to obey God
and keep His Commandments.
"He who does the will of My Father Who is in Heaven," Jesus
said, "he shall enter into the kingdom of Heaven."
God the Father wants us to obey His Ten Commandments.

Jesus teaches us that we must love God with all our mind, heart,
soul, and strength.

We must love our neighbor as ourselves.

We must keep His Commandments.

Jesus cured many who were ill.

Jesus and His Teachings

Jesus taught us how to pray.
Jesus showed us that it is important to pray.
Jesus was once asked how to pray.
Jesus taught us a prayer. We call this prayer the Our Father.

When we say:
"Our Father Who art in Heaven,"
Jesus wants all of us to think about God as our loving Father.
Jesus wants us to call God "Our Father"
whenever we pray to Him.
God is with us wherever we are.
But Jesus reminds us that there is a special place
which is God's home. That place is Heaven.
We want to go to Heaven someday to be with God Who loves us.

Jesus taught us how to pray.

"Hallowed be Thy name."
Here Jesus teaches us that the name of God is holy.
Since God's name is so holy, we must be sure to use it in a special respectful way.

"Thy Kingdom Come."
With these words, we tell God that we want the truth
and good of His Heavenly kingdom here on earth also.
Jesus is our King. Someday, we all will see Him as the King of Kings.

"Thy Will be done on earth as it is in Heaven."
In this part of the prayer, Jesus teaches us to pray that we always do the will of God, that what God wants in Heaven, is done on earth.
Whatever God wants on earth should be done.
When we obey the Ten Commandments, we are doing the will of God.
Jesus says to us: **If you love Me, keep My Commandments.**

Martyrs in the Catacombs

Jesus and His Teachings

Jesus taught us His Commandment of Love.
His Commandment of Love is:

Thou shalt love the Lord thy God with thy whole heart, and with thy whole soul, with thy whole mind and with thy whole strength. "This is the greatest and first commandment," He said. "The other is: **Thou shalt love thy neighbor as thyself.**"

Jesus is the Good Shepherd.

These two Great Commandments are a simple way
of saying the Ten Commandments.
The first three Commandments are about our duties to God.
To love God with everything we have
sums up the first three Commandments.

The last seven Commandments are about our duties to our neighbor.
To love your neighbor as yourself means that just as you must love
and do what is good for yourself, you must love and do what is good
for your neighbor as well.

We can help our neighbor to be good if we are good.
We should be a good example to our neighbor.
The more we know, love, and serve God, the more we can
help our neighbor to know, love, and serve God, too.

The Good Samaritan

Jesus and His Teachings

What is the main teaching of the Catholic Church about Jesus Christ?

The main teaching of the Catholic Church about Jesus Christ is that He is God made man.

What is the prayer that Jesus taught us to pray?

The prayer that Jesus taught us to pray is the Our Father.

What is the greatest and First Commandment of God?

The greatest and First Commandment of God is: Thou shalt love the Lord Thy God with thy whole heart, and with thy whole soul, with thy whole mind, and with thy whole strength.

What is the commandment which sums up the commandments about our neighbor?

"Thou shalt love thy neighbor as thyself" sums up the commandments about our neighbor.

Jesus told the rich young man to obey the Commandments.

Grace and the Sacraments

The Birth of Jesus

Jesus, the Son of God,
came to this world to open the gates of Heaven for us.

God the Father promised Adam and Eve
He would send them a Savior.
When Adam and Eve sinned, God the Father
closed the gates of Heaven.
But God so loved us, that He sent His beloved Son, Jesus.

Jesus came to this world to help us.
Jesus taught us that we must be good to get to Heaven.
We must obey the Ten Commandments.

Jesus gave us help to obey His Commandments.
He gave us seven Sacraments, which give us Grace.
Jesus gave us His Holy Catholic Church
to give us His Sacraments.

Grace and the Sacraments

Jesus teaches us that to get to Heaven,
we must obey the Ten Commandments.
Jesus knows that we need help to obey His Ten Commandments.

Some of us are tempted to steal.
Some of us are tempted to lie.
Some children might talk back to their parents.
Some children do not want to be obedient all the time.
So Jesus showed us a way to help us to be strong so we can be good.
He gives us the gift of Grace.

Grace is a special gift from God.
We cannot see Grace because it helps our invisible souls.
God gives us Grace often to strengthen us and to help us to be good.

Jesus gave us seven Sacraments to give us Grace to make us holy.
All seven Sacraments give us Sanctifying Grace.
The first Sacrament you received was the Sacrament of Baptism.

The seven Sacraments are:

1. Baptism

2. Penance or Reconciliation

3. Holy Eucharist

4. Confirmation

5. Matrimony

6. Holy Orders

7. Anointing of the Sick or Extreme Unction

Grace and the Sacraments

Jesus gave us seven Sacraments to give us Grace to make us holy.

During the three years Jesus taught, Jesus used many signs and acts when He performed miracles. For example, He touched the eyes of those He healed of blindness.
Jesus gave us the Seven Sacraments as outward signs,
so we could see and hear that we are receiving His Grace.

A Sacrament is an outward sign given to us by Jesus to give us Grace.
For example, in the Sacrament of Baptism,
water is poured over the head of the person to be baptized, and
the priest says the words:
"I baptize you in the Name of the Father, and of the Son,
and of the Holy Spirit." The water and the words are signs we
can see and hear of the
Grace we are receiving
during Baptism.

In the Sacrament of the
Holy Eucharist, the host is
the outward sign. When the
proper words are said by
the priest, the bread
and wine become the Body
and Blood of Jesus Christ.

When we receive the
Sacraments, we receive
Sanctifying Grace.
Sanctifying Grace makes us
holy and pleasing to God.
Sanctifying Grace makes us
children of God.

St. John the Baptist baptizes Jesus

Grace and the Sacraments

Did the Son of God come to earth to open the gates of Heaven?
   Yes, the Son of God came to earth to open the gates of Heaven.

Why were the gates of Heaven closed?
   The gates of Heaven were closed because of the sin of Adam and Eve.

Did God our Heavenly Father promise to send a Savior?
   Yes, God our Heavenly Father promised to send a Savior, His Son
   Jesus Christ, to open the gates of Heaven.

Jesus came to open the gates of Heaven.

Did Jesus show us how to get to Heaven?
   Yes, Jesus showed us how to get to Heaven. He said to obey the Ten
   Commandments.

**What did Jesus give us to help us obey the Ten
Commandments?**
   Jesus helps us obey the Ten Commandments by giving us
   Sanctifying Grace.

What is Sanctifying Grace?

Sanctifying Grace is an invisible gift from God for our souls.

What is a Sacrament?

A Sacrament is an outward sign given to us by Jesus Christ to give us Grace.

The apostles receive Communion.

How do we get Sanctifying Grace?

We get Sanctifying Grace when we receive the Sacraments.

Why did Jesus give us the sacraments?

Jesus gave us the sacraments to give us Sanctifying Grace.

What does Sanctifying Grace do for our souls?

Sanctifying Grace makes our souls holy and pleasing to God.

Does Sanctifying Grace make us children of God?

Yes, Sanctifying Grace makes us children of God.

The Sacrament of Baptism

You have received at least one Sacrament, the Sacrament of Baptism. Baptism is such an important Sacrament that it is given to Catholic babies as soon as possible after birth.

We call Adam and Eve our first parents.
When Adam and Eve sinned, they committed the first sin.
We call that first sin, Original Sin.

All of us on earth inherit Original Sin from our first parents.
When Adam and Eve sinned, they lost Grace.
All of us are born with Original Sin.
All of us are born without Sanctifying Grace.
All of us are born unable to go to Heaven.

Baptism of Jesus

The Sacrament of Baptism

Jesus gave us the Sacrament of Baptism to take away Original Sin.
Jesus gave us the Sacrament of Baptism to give us Sanctifying Grace.
Jesus gave us the Sacrament of Baptism so we could go to Heaven.

Baptism is the Sacrament that gives our souls
the new Life of Grace by which we become children of God.
Baptism takes away Original Sin.

God knew the Blessed Virgin Mary
would always choose to do His holy Will.
God gave her the special gift of Sanctifying Grace.
The Blessed Virgin Mary is FULL of Grace.

The Blessed Mother never had Original Sin.
The Blessed Virgin Mary's soul was full of Grace
from the first instant of her creation.

Baptism of Jesus

The Sacrament of Baptism

Jesus wants all of us to go to Heaven.
Jesus wants us to be happy with Him in Heaven.
He gave us the Sacrament of Baptism to help us to go to Heaven.
He gave us the Sacrament of Baptism to take away Original Sin.
He gave us the Sacrament of Baptism to
give us Sanctifying Grace.
The Sacrament of Baptism washes away Original Sin
from our soul and fills it with the Grace of God.

When we are baptized, we become members
of the Catholic Church.
God our Heavenly Father adopts us as His children.
Jesus loves us as His own brothers and sisters.
Jesus gives us His Mother to be our Heavenly Mother.

To give us the Sacrament of Baptism, Jesus Christ Himself
was baptized by St. John the Baptist in the River Jordan.

When Jesus was baptized, as He
"came out of the water,
the heavens were opened to Him:
and He saw the Spirit of God
descending as a dove, and coming
upon Him.
And a voice from Heaven saying:
This is My beloved Son, in Whom
I am well pleased."

Jesus commanded all to receive
the Sacrament of Baptism.

Jesus gives us a beautiful gift of
Supernatural Grace when we are
baptized. Without Grace, we
cannot go to Heaven.

Baptism of Jesus

The Sacrament of Baptism

Baptism of Jesus by John the Baptist

Jesus gave us the Sacrament of Baptism.
He gave us the Sacrament of Baptism to take away Original Sin.
We inherit Original Sin from Adam and Eve.

Jesus wants us to have Sanctifying Grace in our souls.
Jesus wants us to go to Heaven.
We need Sanctifying Grace to go to Heaven.
So Jesus gave us the Sacrament of Baptism.

Baptism also makes us members of the Catholic Church.
Baptism makes us children of God.
After Baptism, the home of our Father in Heaven is opened to us.

Our mother and our father take care of us on earth.
They show us how to be good.
They teach us about Jesus.

Our parents teach us about God our Father in Heaven.
Our parents love us and God very, very much.
Someday all who love God will be happy
forever with Him in Heaven.

The Sacrament of Baptism

What sin do we inherit from our first parents, Adam and Eve?
The sin we inherit from our first parents is Original Sin.

Was anyone ever free from Original Sin?
Yes, the Blessed Virgin Mary was free from Original Sin.

What is a Sacrament?
A Sacrament is an outward sign given to us by Jesus Christ to give us Grace.

What Sacrament have you received?
I have received the Sacrament of Baptism.

What did Baptism do for you?
Baptism removed Original Sin from my soul and gave me Sanctifying Grace.

What does Sanctifying Grace do for my soul?
Sanctifying Grace makes my soul holy and pleasing to God.

Baptism of Jesus

The Sacrament of Penance

One of the Sacraments you are preparing to receive is the Sacrament of Penance or Reconciliation. Catholic children usually receive this Sacrament when they are seven or eight years old.

The Sacrament of Penance or Reconciliation is the Sacrament by which sins committed after Baptism are forgiven. The Sacrament of Penance is also called Confession.

The Sacrament of Penance was given to us by Jesus Christ. Jesus gave His twelve apostles the power to forgive sins. The apostles were the first Catholic bishops.
All Catholic bishops, beginning with the apostles, have the power to forgive sins.

Bishops can ordain new bishops or priests who then have the power to forgive sins.

The priest who forgives you your sins represents Jesus Christ.

Jesus Christ

When you hear the priest forgive you your sins, it is a true sign to you that God forgives your sins. Sins are forgiven by Jesus through the priest in the Sacrament of Penance.

The Sacrament of Penance

The Sacrament of Penance is the Sacrament that takes away my sins. It is the Sacrament by which the sins I commit after Baptism are forgiven. I must receive the Sacrament of Penance before I receive my First Holy Communion.

I receive the Sacrament of Penance each time I go to Confession. A priest gives me the Sacrament of Penance when I go to Confession.

In the Sacrament of Penance, God gives me Sanctifying Grace. Sanctifying Grace makes me holy and pleasing to God.
Even if I have Sanctifying Grace, I receive more when I receive the Sacrament of Penance.

If I have lost Sanctifying Grace, God restores it to my soul through the Sacrament of Penance.
The Sacrament of Penance makes me holy and pleasing to God.
That is why many Catholics go to Confession frequently. The pope goes to Confession every day!

In the Sacrament of Penance, sins committed after Baptism are forgiven.

Baptism

The Sacrament of Penance

Jesus worked many miracles during His public life.
Jesus cured the sick and they became well instantly.
Jesus cured the crippled and they walked.
Jesus cured those who were blind and they could see.
Jesus cured those who were deaf and they could hear.

Many loved Jesus because He showed them how much He loved them.
But He did something even greater than curing the sick.
He forgave sins.

When someone is sick or crippled, we wish they were well.
Jesus showed us that sin is worse than being sick or crippled.
Sin makes the soul blind to God.
Sin makes the soul unable to hear God.
Sin makes the soul ugly and weak.
Sin is much worse than disease, cold, or flu.

It is easy for us to see how sick people are weak and helpless.
But God sees how sin makes our souls sick and weak.
It is easy for God to work a miracle to cure someone who is sick.
But, most of all, God wants to cure souls of the weakness sin makes
in them.

One time, some men brought their friend, a crippled man, to Jesus. The
man could not walk. Many thought that Jesus would help the man to
walk.
But Jesus said to the man: "Be of good heart, Son, your sins are forgiven
you."
Jesus knows that when our sins are forgiven, we are happy.
We have a special wonderful peace when our sins are forgiven.
The sacrament of Confession makes us strong in virtue, beautiful in
Grace, and pleasing to God.

The Sacrament of Penance

The apostles were given the power to forgive sins.

What is the Sacrament of Penance?

Penance is the Sacrament by which sins committed after Baptism are forgiven.

Who gave us the Sacrament of Penance?

Jesus gave us the Sacrament of Penance.

Who was given the power to forgive sins?

The apostles were given the power to forgive sins.

Who has the power today to forgive sins?

Priests have the power to forgive sins.

Besides taking away our sins, what else does the Sacrament of Penance do for us?

Besides taking away our sins, the Sacrament of Penance gives us Sanctifying Grace.

Sin

Sin is an offense against God.
Sin is disobedience to the laws of God.
Sin is breaking one of the commandments of God.
God gave us the Ten Commandments so that we can be happy.
Sin robs our soul of Grace.

If we disobey one of the Ten Commandments, we commit a sin.

If we keep the Ten Commandments, we show that we love God.

When we obey the Commandments of God, we give Him glory.

We can be happy and have peace if we obey God's commandments.

Sin is turning away from God.

We tell Him by our sin that we do not love Him.

God wants me to love Him.

Jesus died for us.

When I sin, I do not act the way God wants me to act. I am not being loving to God.

When we obey God's laws, we are being good.

When we disobey God's laws, we do wrong.

When we disobey God's laws, we sin.

Sin

We are being good when we obey God's laws.
We are not being good when we disobey God's laws.
If we commit a bad act, we offend God.

When we sin, it is called an actual sin.
When we do a bad act, we commit an actual sin.
We inherit Original Sin from Adam and Eve.
Adam and Eve committed the First Sin, which we call Original Sin.

Actual sins are sins we ourselves commit.
There are two kinds of actual sin:

MORTAL SIN

and

VENIAL SIN

We must be sorry for our sins because they offend God.

We must be sorry for our sins because they offend God.

Sin

Sin is disobeying the laws of God.
Sin is an offense against God's infinite Goodness.
A bad act we commit is called a sin.

Actual sins are sins we ourselves commit.
There are two kinds of actual sin: mortal sin and venial sin.

Mortal sin is a very bad sin.
Mortal sin takes away all the Grace that was in our soul.
Mortal sin offends God by showing Him we really love something else more than we love God.
Mortal sin is very serious sin.

Anyone who dies in mortal sin cannot go to Heaven.
We must try very, very hard never to commit a mortal sin.

Venial sin is bad, but it is less of an offense against God.
Venial sin is a lesser sin.
Venial sin displeases God, too.
Venial sin makes us unhappy, too.

We must try not to commit even venial sins.
We must love God above all things to be happy.

The Immaculate Conception

Sin

What is sin?

Sin is disobeying God's laws.

Is Original Sin the only kind of sin?

No, there is another kind of sin called actual sin.

What is actual sin?

Actual sin is any sin that we ourselves commit.

How many kinds of actual sin are there?

There are two kinds of actual sin: mortal sin and venial sin.

What is mortal sin?

Mortal sin is a very serious sin.

What does mortal sin do to us?

Mortal sin makes us enemies of God and robs our soul of His Grace.

What is venial sin?

Venial sin is a lesser sin.

Does venial sin displease God?

Yes, venial sin does displease God.

Does venial sin rob our souls of His Grace?

No, venial sin does not rob our souls of His Grace.

Confession

Penance is the Sacrament that takes away my sins.
The Sacrament of Penance gives me the Grace to do good.
To receive the Sacrament of Penance, I must tell my sins to a priest.
Confession is the telling of my sins to a priest to have them forgiven.
I receive the Sacrament of Penance when I go to Confession.

Jesus knows when I sin.
Jesus knows when I am sorry for my sins.
But Jesus wants us to show Him we are sorry.
Jesus wants us to tell the priest that we are sorry for our sins.

After Jesus rose from the dead on the first Easter, He told His apostles:
"Whose sins you shall forgive, they are forgiven; and whose sins you shall not forgive, they are not forgiven."

Jesus gave His apostles, and all the other priests, the power to forgive sins in His Name. Jesus forgives us our sins when we hear the priest forgive us in Confession.

All mortal sins must be told to the priest in Confession.
Jesus will forgive mortal sins when we tell them to the priest in Confession.

Doubting Thomas

Confession

Jesus gave us the Sacrament of Penance to heal the sickness sin causes in our souls. He also gave us the Sacrament of Penance to give us Grace to help us to keep the Commandments.

To receive the Sacrament of Penance, we must go to Confession. Confession is necessary to remove our very serious sins. Confession is important also to obtain graces to be good.

Most children receive the Sacrament of Penance when they are about six or seven years old.

The son of the widow from Nain is raised from the dead.

To make a good confession, I must do five things:

1. Find out my sins.
2. Be sorry for my sins.
3. Make up my mind not to sin again.
4. Tell my sins to the priest.
5. Do the penance the priest gives me.

The most important part of Confession is being sorry for my sins. Sin offends God Who is all Good and worthy of all my love.

Confession

Confession is the telling of my sins to a priest to have them forgiven.
Jesus wants us to confess our sins to a priest.
In Confession, the priest uses the power which Jesus gives him.
The priest takes the place of Jesus in the confessional.

When I tell my sins to the priest in the confessional,
I am really telling them to Jesus.

I make my Confession in this way:

1. I go into the confessional and kneel.
2. I make the Sign of the Cross and say:
    "Bless me, Father, for I have sinned."
3. I say: "This is my first confession."
    Or say how long it has been since my last confession.
4. I confess my sins to the priest.
5. I listen to what the priest tells me.
6. I say the Act of Contrition loud enough
    for the priest to hear me.
7. I say "Thank you, Father, God bless you."
8. I leave the confessional and say the prayers the priest
    gives me for my penance before leaving the church.

St. John Nepomucene hears confessions.

Confession

What must you do to receive the Sacrament of Penance?

To receive the Sacrament of Penance, I must:

1. Find out my sins.
2. Be sorry for my sins.
3. Make up my mind not to sin again.
4. Tell my sins to the priest.
5. Do the penance the priest gives me.

How do you make your confession?

I make my confession in this way:

1. I go into the confessional and kneel.
2. I make the Sign of the Cross and say: "Bless me, Father, for I have sinned."
3. Then I say "This is my first confession."
   Or I say how long it has been since my last confession.
4. I confess my sins.
5. I listen to what the priest tells me.
6. I say the Act of Contrition loud enough for the priest to hear me.
7. I say: "Thank you, Father, God bless you."

What do you do after leaving the confessional?

After leaving the confessional, I say the penance the priest has given me, and thank God for forgiving my sins.

St. John Nepomucene hears confessions.

The Sacrament of Matrimony

Jesus wants us to know that being married is very important.
So Jesus made getting married a Sacrament.
Jesus gave us the Sacrament of Matrimony.

When a man and a woman love each other and want to be married, they must give their promise to stay married in church in front of a priest and witnesses.

This Sacrament gives Grace to the bride and groom.
The Sacrament of Matrimony helps the married couple to love and to live together in holiness, and to raise their children to be holy.

The first public miracle that Jesus worked was at a wedding. Many people believe that Jesus worked His first miracle at a wedding because He wants us to see the importance of marriage and the family. It was the Wedding Feast at Cana.
Jesus changed water into wine at the Wedding Feast of Cana.

Like every other Sacrament, Matrimony is an outward sign, something visible that we can see, that Christ Himself made for us to give us Grace.
The Sacrament of Matrimony helps the bride and groom and their family to live in love and holiness.

Wedding Feast at Cana

The Sacrament of Matrimony

Jesus made marriage a Sacrament because He wants parents to teach and train their children to know, love, and serve God.

The Sacrament of Matrimony helps a man and a woman to become holy, to love each other, and to teach their children to be holy.

Jesus loves little children in a special way.
One time, Jesus was surrounded by little children.
His apostles tried to push the children away.
The apostles were afraid the children were bothering Jesus.

Jesus said:

"Let the little children come to Me,

For of such is the kingdom of Heaven."

Children are eager to learn the truth about everything.
God our Father sent Jesus to teach all God's children the truth.
Someday, we all hope to be with our Father in Heaven forever.

Know, love and serve God with all your mind, heart, soul, and strength.
Show God you love Him by keeping His Commandments.
After the first three commandments, the Fourth Commandment
is the most important:

Honor thy father and thy mother.

The Sacrament of Matrimony

Jesus made marriage a Sacrament.
He made marriage a Sacrament so that parents will have a special supernatural help from God to love each other and to become holy together and to do what God wants to help their children become holy.

Jesus wants parents to take care of their children.
Jesus wants parents to teach their children all about God.
Jesus wants parents to teach their children to love Him and obey God's laws. Children need their parents to teach them about God's laws.

When a couple receives the Sacrament of Matrimony, they promise to stay together until one of them dies.
They promise to be good and live a holy life together.

The Marriage of Mary and Joseph

When a couple receives the Sacrament of Matrimony, they show God and each other that they are happy to have the children God sends them.
They show that they love God and each other and that they will raise any children God gives them, to know, love, and serve Him.

The Sacrament of Matrimony

Jesus made marriage a Sacrament to help a man and a woman who marry.
Jesus loves little children.
Jesus loves families.
He loves parents and their children.

Jesus is very happy when parents and children go to Mass together.
Jesus is very happy when parents and children learn about God together.

Jesus was born in a family because He wanted to show us how important it is to be a good and loving family.
Jesus, Mary, and Joseph are the Holy Family.

We call God our Father because He is our Father in Heaven.
We call the Blessed Virgin Mary our Mother because she is our heavenly mother.

God wants our family to be like the Holy Family.
God wants our family to be loving and holy.

Jesus, Mary, and Joseph are the Holy Family.

The Sacrament of Matrimony gives Grace to a husband and wife.
Grace gives them help to love each other.
Grace helps them to raise the children God sends them.

WEEK TWENTY-SEVEN: DAY 1

Please review the Catechism and Catechism questions and answers for weeks 1 to 8.
Ask your child to give you the Catechism answers as accurately as possible.

WEEK TWENTY-SEVEN: Day 2

Please review the Catechism and Catechism questions and answers for weeks 10 to 17.
Ask your child to give you the Catechism answers as accurately as possible.

WEEK TWENTY-SEVEN: Day 3

Please review the Catechism and Catechism questions and answers for weeks 19 to 22.
Ask your child to give you the Catechism answers as accurately as possible.

WEEK TWENTY-SEVEN: Day 4

Please review the Catechism and Catechism questions and answers for weeks 23 to 26.
Ask your child to give you the Catechism answers as accurately as possible.

"Let the children come to Me!"

The Sacrament of the Holy Eucharist

Jesus gave us seven Sacraments.
The greatest Sacrament is the Sacrament of the Holy Eucharist.
This is the greatest of all the Sacraments
because it is Jesus Himself.

That's right!
Jesus gives us Himself in the Sacrament of the Holy Eucharist.

The Last Supper

Jesus gave His priests the power
to change bread and wine into His Body and Blood.
When we receive Holy Communion,
we are receiving Jesus in the Sacrament of the Holy Eucharist.

St. John wrote in his Gospel in the Bible what Jesus said:
"But My Father gives you the True Bread from Heaven.
I Am the Bread of Life: he that comes to Me shall not hunger,
and he that believes in Me shall never thirst."

Jesus said: "This is the Bread that came down from Heaven.
Not like the manna your fathers ate and are dead.
He that eats this Bread, shall live forever."

"He that eats this Bread, shall live forever."

The Sacrament of the Holy Eucharist

Jesus gave us the Sacrament of the Holy Eucharist at the Last Supper. This was the Last Supper Jesus had with His apostles before He died.

The Last Supper

While they were eating, Jesus took bread, blessed it, broke it, and gave it to the apostles. He said, "This is My Body."
The apostles received the Body of Jesus
under the appearance of bread.

Jesus then took a chalice filled with wine, and giving thanks, He blessed it and said to them, "This is My Blood."
The apostles drank the Blood of Jesus
under the appearance of wine.
Jesus told His apostles: "Do this in memory of Me."

The Last Supper was the First Communion of the apostles.
It was the time that Jesus chose to give us His greatest Miracle.
Jesus is still with us on earth in a hidden way,
even after He died, rose, and ascended into Heaven.
He is with us in Holy Communion.

The Sacrament of the Holy Eucharist

At the Last Supper, Jesus Christ, Who is God,
changed bread and wine into His Body and Blood.
Jesus said: "This is My Body" and the bread became His Body.
Then Jesus said: "This is My Blood"
and the wine became His Blood.

The bread and wine changed into the Body
and Blood of Jesus Christ.
Our Lord Jesus Christ gave the apostles
their First Holy Communion.
Jesus told the apostles to continue to do what He had done.

Jesus gave the apostles the power to change the bread and wine
into the Body and Blood of Jesus Christ
when they say the words of consecration.
Each time the priest says the words of Consecration during the Mass,
he is doing what Jesus did.

When we go to Mass, the priest changes the bread and wine
into the Body and Blood of Jesus Christ.
At Mass, Jesus Christ becomes truly Present
in the Holy Eucharist.

The Holy Eucharist is really and truly Jesus Christ,
Who comes into our hearts when we receive Him at Mass.
The Host looks like bread, and tastes like bread.
But the Holy Eucharist is really Jesus.

The Holy Eucharist is Jesus.
Jesus gives Himself to me in the Most Holy Eucharist.
Through the Holy Eucharist, Jesus actually lives in me!

The Sacrament of the Holy Eucharist

What is the Sacrament of the Holy Eucharist?

The Sacrament of the Holy Eucharist is the Sacrament of the Body and Blood of Our Lord Jesus Christ.

When did Christ give us the Sacrament of the Holy Eucharist?

Christ gave us the Holy Eucharist at the Last Supper, the night before He died.

What did Our Lord do at the Last Supper?

At the Last Supper, Our Lord Jesus Christ changed bread and wine into His Body and Blood.

"This is My Body."

How could Jesus change bread and wine into His Body and Blood?

Our Lord Jesus Christ could do this because He is God, and God can do all things.

When does Jesus Christ become present in the Holy Eucharist?

Jesus Christ becomes present in the Holy Eucharist during the Mass when the priest says, "This is My Body" and "This is My Blood."

Who were with Our Lord Jesus Christ at the Last Supper?

The apostles were with Our Lord Jesus Christ at the Last Supper.

Did Our Lord give the apostles and all the priests of the Catholic Church the power to change bread and wine into His Body and Blood?

Yes, Our Lord gave the apostles and all the priests of the Catholic Church the power to change bread and wine into His Body and Blood.

When do the priests use this power?

The priests use this power when they offer the Holy Mass and say the words of consecration: "This is My Body" and "This is My Blood."

Jesus at the Last Supper

Holy Communion

**I receive Jesus in the Sacrament of the Holy Eucharist
when I receive Holy Communion.**

Since Jesus is true God and true Man, He can be in Heaven with the
saints and also be on earth with us.
Jesus loves us so much He made a Miracle so He could be with us.

The whole Jesus, His Body, Blood, Soul, and Divinity,
is Present in the Holy Eucharist in a hidden manner.

The apostles receive Communion.

Every day at Mass, Jesus becomes physically and entirely Present. Jesus remains hidden under the appearances of bread and wine.

When a man receives the Sacrament of Holy Orders, he becomes a priest with the very special power to change the bread and wine into the Body and Blood of Jesus.

Jesus is God.

Jesus is with us on earth in the Sacrament of the Holy Eucharist. Jesus loves us.

He wants to help us to be good. So Jesus comes to us Body, Blood, Soul, and Divinity in the Holy Eucharist.

Jesus at the Last Supper

Holy Communion

One day, Jesus told a crowd:

I Am the Bread of Life.

The Holy Eucharist is the living Body and Blood of Jesus Christ.
Jesus is truly Present in the Holy Eucharist.
We receive Him in Holy Communion.

Jesus loves me.
Jesus wants to come to me often in Holy Communion.
I need to prepare myself
to receive Jesus.

I say the prayers at Mass.
During the Mass, I tell Jesus I
am sorry for my sins.

Tell Jesus you love Him as
often as you can.
Ask your Guardian Angel to
help you to tell Jesus you love
Him.
Tell Jesus you want Him to
come into your heart.

Holy Communion protects us
from sin.
Jesus draws us closer to
Himself and away from sin.
Jesus makes us strong to
resist sin.

*Jesus wants to come to me often
in Holy Communion.*

Jesus helps our minds to know what is true.
Jesus helps our wills to choose what is good for us.

If you have not made your First Holy Communion yet,
Jesus will come to you in a Spiritual Communion if you ask Him.

Holy Communion

At Mass, the Host is small and round and white.
It looks and tastes like bread, but the Host is not bread.
It is Jesus.

It looks and tastes like bread,
but after the priest says the words of consecration,
"This is My Body,"
It is not bread.
It is Jesus.

The wine looks like wine.
It may smell and
taste like wine.
But after the priest says the
words of consecration,
"This is My Blood,"
It is not wine.
It is Jesus.

I cannot see Jesus.
Jesus is hidden under the
appearance of bread and wine.
But Jesus is there.
Jesus taught that He is truly
and really Present.
Jesus is God. What He says is
true.
We call this miracle of Jesus
the Real Presence.

Jesus said, "This is My Body."
Jesus said, "This is My Blood."
Jesus is God.
What He says is true.

"This is My Body."

Holy Communion

What is Holy Communion?

Holy Communion is the receiving of Our Lord's Body and Blood in the Sacrament of the Holy Eucharist.

Do you see Jesus Christ in the Holy Eucharist?

No, I do not see Jesus Christ in the Holy Eucharist because He is hidden under the appearances of bread and wine.

When does Jesus become present in the Holy Eucharist?

Jesus Christ becomes present in the Holy Eucharist during the Mass when the priest says, "This is My Body" and "This is My Blood."

"This is My Body" and "This is My Blood"

What must you do to receive Holy Communion worthily?

To receive Holy Communion worthily, I must have my soul free from mortal sin.

What should I do before receiving Jesus in Holy Communion?

Before receiving Jesus in Holy Communion, I should:

1. Tell Jesus I am sorry for my sins.
2. Thank Jesus for coming to me in Holy Communion.
3. Tell Jesus I want Him to come to me.

What should I do after receiving Jesus in Holy Communion?

After receiving Jesus in Holy Communion, I should:

Adore Jesus by saying, "My Lord and My God."
Love Jesus and tell Him how much I love Him.
Thank Jesus for coming to me and for all His blessings.
Ask Jesus to help me and everyone in my family.
Repair — Offer Jesus my Communion to repair for my sins and the sins of others.

The Last Supper

Jesus Dies for Us

Sin came into the world when Adam and Eve committed the first sin.
God the Father closed the gates of Heaven.
God the Father promised Adam and Eve that He would send a Savior.
God the Father sent His only-begotten Son, Jesus,
to die for our sins and to open the gates of Heaven.

After the Last Supper, soldiers came and took Jesus to be put to death.
No greater gift can a person give than his own life for someone else.
Jesus gave His life to show us how much He loves us.

The Kiss of Judas

Jesus suffered for us before He died.

He was spit upon.

He was beaten.

A crown of thorns was put on the Sacred Head of Jesus.

Jesus gave His own life on the Cross to open the gates of Heaven.
Jesus offered His sufferings and death on the Cross
to God the Father to make up for all our sins.

The Crowning of Thorns

By dying on the Cross, Jesus opened the gates of Heaven.

Now the gates of Heaven are open to us.

When we die, if we are sorry for our sins, we can go to Heaven.

Jesus Dies for Us

When Adam and Eve, our first parents, were disobedient to God the Father, He closed the gates of Heaven. But God promised to send a Savior to open the gates of Heaven.

God the Father sent His Son, Jesus Christ, to save us.
Jesus saved us by dying on the Cross for us.
Jesus loved us so much that He came to earth to save us.
When Jesus died on the Cross, God the Father opened the gates of Heaven.

Before Jesus came, God's people offered sacrifices to God.
God's people offered sacrifices of their animals, such as a little lamb.
God's people offered sacrifices of food they had grown, such as the best fruit and vegetables and flowers.

Jesus saved us by dying on the Cross for us.

They wanted to show God that the sacrifice was not for themselves, but for God. They would take their gift for God to the priest and he would kill it the way God commanded Moses. They would burn it so that it was completely destroyed. This was called a sacrifice.

But these gifts and sacrifices were not good enough to open the gates of Heaven.
Jesus is the Second Person of the Blessed Trinity.
Jesus became man to offer a Perfect Sacrifice to God for sin.
God the Father in Heaven accepted His Son as a Sacrifice for sin.
Because Jesus died for us, God the Father opened the gates of Heaven.

Jesus Dies for Us

Jesus died on the Cross as a Sacrifice to God the Father for our sins.

Jesus died on the Cross for us to open the gates of Heaven.

The Holy Sacrifice of the Mass is the same but unbloody Sacrifice of Jesus on the Cross. In every Holy Mass, Jesus Christ offers Himself as a Sacrifice on the Cross for us.

In every Holy Mass, the priest offers Jesus to God the Father as a Sacrifice.

The priest says the prayers of the Mass. When the priest says the words of Jesus, the bread and wine are changed into the Body and Blood of Jesus.

Jesus died on the Cross as a Sacrifice to God.

The Body and Blood of Jesus is the Perfect Sacrifice to God the Father.

The Mass is the Sacrifice in which Jesus, through the priest, offers Himself to God under the appearance of bread and wine. In the Holy Sacrifice of the Mass, Jesus offers Himself up for our sins.

Jesus Dies for Us

What is the Mass?

The Mass is the unbloody Sacrifice in which Jesus Christ, through the priest, offers Himself to God under the appearances of bread and wine.

Why did Jesus Christ die on the Cross?

Jesus Christ died on the Cross to offer His sufferings and death to God the Father in satisfaction for the sins of man.

What do we learn from the sufferings and death of Christ?

From the sufferings and death of Christ, we learn God's love for us, and the evil of sin.

Jesus died on the Cross to offer His sufferings and death to God the Father.

The Resurrection of Jesus

Jesus died on the Cross for us on Good Friday,
but Jesus rose from the dead on Easter Sunday morning.

The third day after His death, Jesus rose from the dead!
On Easter Sunday morning, all the apostles were surprised.
Jesus rose from the dead!
Jesus rose from the dead with a glorious and immortal Body.

On Easter Sunday morning, Mary Magdalen and other holy women
went to the tomb of Jesus.
They went to anoint the Body of Jesus with sweet spices.

The Resurrection

When they arrived, the heavy stone sealing the tomb had been thrown aside! With great courage, they approached the tomb and near the entrance, they saw an Angel seated upon the heavy stone. The Angel looked like a young man whose face shone brighter than the sun and whose garments were whiter than snow. The Angel said to them, "Do not be afraid. You seek Jesus of Nazareth, Who was crucified. He is not here. Come and see the place where the Lord was laid."

The Holy Women at the Tomb

Mary Magdalen and the holy women saw the empty tomb. The Angel continued: "Why do you seek the Living with the dead? Remember what He told you when He was yet in Galilee, that He was to rise on the third day. Go tell His disciples and Peter that He goes before you into Galilee. There you shall see Him, just as He told you."

Mary Magdalen and the holy women left the tomb. They were trembling with fear. They said nothing to anyone before they told Peter and the apostles what they had seen and heard.

The Resurrection of Jesus

Mary Magdalen ran to the Upper Room where the apostles were hiding in fear. They rushed to tell Peter what had happened to the women at Jesus' tomb. On hearing that the tomb was empty, both Peter and John ran back to the tomb to see for themselves what Mary Magdalen had reported. Mary Magdalen also rushed back to the tomb with them.

Peter and John ran and ran to the tomb. John was younger and reached it first, but he waited for Peter since Peter was the head of all the apostles. While John was waiting for Peter to catch up, John peered into the tomb without going in and saw the linen cloth that had been Jesus' shroud lying there. Peter arrived shortly and went into the tomb. He also saw the linen cloths in which Jesus had been buried lying there folded. He saw the special cloth that had been around Jesus' head not lying with the linen shroud but wrapped up and set aside in another place. Then John went in and saw and believed.

Mary Magdalen runs into the Upper Room.

Neither Peter nor John had seen the risen Jesus Himself yet. They still did not fully understand that the Son of God must rise from the dead. However, they returned to the Upper Room and reported that what the holy women had told the apostles there earlier about the tomb being empty was true. Peter wondered at all that had happened.

Meanwhile, Mary Magdalen did not understand why the tomb was empty and remained standing outside the tomb weeping. She thought someone had stolen the Body of Jesus. While she was weeping, she stooped down and looked into the entrance of the tomb again now that Peter and John had gone. There she could see

"Woman, why are you weeping?"

two Angels in white, one sitting at the head, and one at the feet where the Body of Jesus had been laid. She went in closer. Each Angel's face was brighter than lightning, and their clothes were as white as snow. The Angels said to her, "Woman, why are you weeping?" Mary said, "Because they have stolen the Body of Jesus. And I don't know where they put Him."

The Resurrection of Jesus

Mary Magdalen turned around, and saw Jesus standing there. But she did not recognize Jesus. She thought it was the gardener. Jesus said to her, "Woman, why are you weeping? Whom do you seek?"

Mary Magdalen said to Him, "Sir, if you have taken Him someplace, tell me where you have laid Him, and I will take Him away." In a gentle and loving voice, Jesus said to her: "Mary!"

Mary thought Jesus was the gardener.

The instant He said her name, Mary Magdalen recognized it was Jesus. She turned to Jesus with delight and said, "Master!" When Mary Magdalen recognized Jesus alive, she was so happy, she fell down on her knees in front of Him to adore Him. She was about to kiss His feet, those same feet that she once washed with her tears and dried with her hair. But Jesus said to her: "Mary, do not touch Me, for I have not yet ascended to My Father in Heaven. But go to My apostles and say to them: I ascend to My Father and to your Father, to My God and to your God."

As Mary Magdalen left the entrance to the tomb, she met up with the other holy women who had followed Peter and John back to the tomb. She told them that she had seen Jesus risen! They listened with awe and began to leave the tomb area with fear and great joy. They were about to run back to tell the apostles, when Jesus met and greeted them all! All the holy women recognized Him! Jesus said to them: "All hail!" Then the holy women knelt down at His sacred feet and began to worship Him. Then Jesus said to them: "Fear not. Go, tell My brethren that they should go into Galilee, there they shall see Me."

"Mary, do not touch Me..."

Mary Magdalen and the holy women immediately returned to the Upper Room where the apostles were gathered and told them that Jesus was indeed risen and that Jesus Himself had met them and spoken to them.

The Resurrection of Jesus

On Easter Sunday morning, Jesus rose from the dead!
Jesus proved that He is God by His Resurrection from the dead.
Only God could rise from the dead by His own power.

Before His Resurrection, Jesus went to the place where all the holy souls waited after their deaths because the gates of Heaven were closed to them. Now that the gates of Heaven were open, Jesus would take all these saints to Heaven.

Jesus rose from the dead!

The Resurrection of Jesus

St. Matthew writes in his Gospel that many of the saints who had died were united with their bodies briefly after Jesus' Resurrection. They came into Jerusalem and were seen by many people.

Jesus appeared to many people after His Resurrection. He appeared to two disciples walking along the road to the city of Emmaus. They did not recognize Him at first but He explained the Scriptures to them concerning the Son of God and His life and death as a Sacrifice. Then He revealed to them that He was truly Jesus risen from the dead.

Later, Jesus appeared to His apostles in the Upper Room. He came right through the locked doors where the disciples were gathered together because they were afraid. Jesus said to them: "Peace be with you." And then He showed them His hands and His side. Those who were there were very happy to see Jesus again and to know that He was truly risen from the dead.

The Supper at Emmaus

The Resurrection of Jesus

St. Thomas was not with the apostles in the Upper Room when Jesus visited them. When the apostles told him, Thomas did not believe it was Jesus they had seen! Jesus returned a week later and said to Thomas, "Put your fingers in My hands and put your hand into My side. And be not faithless, but believing." Thomas humbly and reverently replied: "My Lord and My God." Jesus then said kindly: "Because you have seen Me, Thomas, you believe. Blessed are they that have not seen, and have believed."

For forty days, Jesus appeared to His apostles and spoke with them about the Kingdom of God. Jesus wanted them to teach all nations about the Son of God and about the things that they had learned from Jesus and what they saw Him say and do.

"My Lord and My God!"

The Resurrection of Jesus

On the fortieth day after His Resurrection, Jesus went with His apostles and disciples to Mount Olivet and ascended into Heaven by His own power. We call this day Ascension Thursday. The last command Jesus gave to His apostles before He ascended was: "Go and teach all nations, baptizing them in the name of the Father, and of the Son, and of the Holy Spirit, and teach them to observe all that I have commanded."

Jesus also gave them a very special promise. Jesus promised that He would be with us all days, even until the end of the world.

When did Jesus Christ rise from the dead?

Jesus Christ rose from the dead on Easter Sunday, the third day after His death.

Why did Jesus Christ rise from the dead?

Jesus Christ rose from the dead to show that He is truly God.

When did Jesus ascend into Heaven?

Jesus ascended Body and Soul into Heaven on Ascension Thursday, forty days after His Resurrection.

Jesus Christ rose from the dead to show that He is truly God.

The Holy Spirit

Before Jesus was born, God taught His people through Abraham, Moses and the Prophets.
We can read about this in the Old Testament.
Then Jesus was born.
Jesus taught His apostles that He is the Son of God.
He taught them that God is His Father.

Jesus also taught His apostles about the Holy Spirit.
The Holy Spirit is the third Divine Person of the Blessed Trinity.
Jesus told His apostles that He would send the Holy Spirit to them after He went back to Heaven.

Jesus told them that after the Holy Spirit came,
they would understand all that He had taught them.
He commanded them to teach in all the lands around Jerusalem.
He commanded them to teach "even to the very ends of the earth."

When Jesus sent the Holy Spirit to them later,
the apostles would understand all that Jesus taught them about God.
When Jesus sent the Holy Spirit to them,
the apostles would no longer be afraid to teach the truth.

The Holy Spirit

The apostles would teach all men that Jesus Christ is God.
The apostles would tell all men that the Kingdom of God had come.
The apostles would no longer be afraid to teach all nations.

The Holy Spirit

The Holy Spirit is the third Person of the Blessed Trinity.

There is only one God.
In God, there are three Divine Persons.
We call this the Blessed Trinity.

God the Father is the first Person of the Blessed Trinity.
God the Son is Jesus Christ, the second Person of the Blessed Trinity.
God the Holy Spirit is the third Person of the Blessed Trinity.

There is only one God.
In God, there are three Divine Persons:
the Father, the Son, and the Holy Spirit.
We call the three Divine Persons in one God the Blessed Trinity.
We know there are three Divine Persons in one God
because Jesus told us.

The Holy Family:
Jesus, Mary, and Joseph

There are three families that are important to me:

The first family important to me is my family on earth:
my father and my mother, my brothers and sisters,
my grandparents and my aunts and uncles.

Another family important to me is the Holy Family:
Jesus, Mary, and Joseph.

A third family important to me is the Family of God:
God the Father, God the Son, and God the Holy Spirit.

The Holy Spirit

When Jesus told His apostles about Himself and about God the Father, He also told them about the Holy Spirit.

Forty days after His Resurrection, Jesus went with His apostles up Mount Olivet in Galilee. Before Jesus ascended into Heaven, He promised to send the Holy Spirit.

Jesus said: "You shall receive the power of the Holy Spirit coming upon you and you shall be witnesses to Me in Jerusalem, and in all Judea, and Samaria, and even to the outermost part of the earth."

The Holy Spirit

And when He had said these things, while the apostles looked on, He was raised up, and a cloud hid Him from their sight.

And while they were watching Him going up to Heaven, two Angels appeared who said to them: 'Why do you stand looking up to Heaven. This Jesus who is taken up from you into Heaven, shall return as you have seen Him going into Heaven.'"

We call the day Jesus ascended into Heaven Ascension Thursday. After Jesus' Ascension into Heaven, the apostles returned to the Upper Room to pray. For nine days, they stayed in the Upper Room praying with the Blessed Mother of Jesus.

On the day we call Pentecost Sunday, the Holy Spirit came. The apostles were all together in the Upper Room when suddenly there came a loud sound from Heaven, as of a mighty wind. The sound of the wind filled the whole house. And there appeared to them parted tongues of fire, and these tongues of fire could be seen above the heads of each one of them. And they were all filled with the Holy Spirit! The Holy Spirit, the third Person of the Blessed Trinity, was with them and in them.

The Holy Spirit

Is there only one God?

Yes, there is only one God.

How many Persons are there in God?

In God, there are three Divine Persons: the Father, the Son, and the Holy Spirit.

What do we call the Three Divine Persons in one God?

We call the three Divine Persons in one God the Blessed Trinity.

How do we know there are three Divine Persons in one God?

We know there are three Divine Persons in one God because we have God's word for it.

When did Jesus ascend into Heaven?

Jesus ascended into Heaven on Ascension Thursday, forty days after His Resurrection.

When did the Holy Spirit come to the apostles?

The Holy Spirit came to the apostles on Pentecost Sunday, fifty days after Jesus rose from the dead, in the form of parted tongues of fire.

Pentecost

Confirmation

Pentecost is a great day in the Catholic Church.
Pentecost was the day that the Holy Spirit came to the apostles.
Pentecost is the birthday of the Church.

The Holy Spirit came in the form of tongues of fire.
The apostles saw these tongues of fire above each apostle's head.
The Holy Spirit brought them a special power, a special Grace.

The apostles were afraid to leave the Upper Room after Jesus died.
They were afraid the soldiers might kill them as they had killed Jesus.

When the Holy Spirit came, He gave them His special power.
They became filled with the Gifts of the Holy Spirit.
They were no longer afraid.
They were filled with Supernatural Grace.
This Grace filled the apostles with a holy courage.
Now they wanted to teach all men about Jesus Christ and His Church.

Pentecost

Confirmation

The apostles received the power of the Holy Spirit on Pentecost Sunday.
They suddenly received the Gifts of the Holy Spirit.
They were not afraid anymore to teach about Jesus and His Church.

On Pentecost, Jesus sent God the Holy Spirit to the apostles.
They were filled with the Holy Spirit.

The Holy Spirit came to them in the form of tongues of fire.
St. Peter was filled with the love of God.
St. Peter spoke to thousands of devout people in the city streets.
St. Peter spoke to them about Jesus.

He told them that Jesus, the Son of God, had been crucified by wicked men.
Jesus had raised Himself from the dead just as God had promised.

The apostles baptized thousands.

Confirmation

The people who heard St. Peter were deeply sorry in their hearts that Jesus had suffered and died on the Cross. They asked St. Peter and the apostles: "What shall we do?"

St. Peter told them: "Do penance and be baptized every one of you, in the Name of Jesus Christ, so that your sins can be taken away, and you shall receive the gift of the Holy Spirit."

St. Peter told them many more things about Jesus and begged his listeners to: "Save yourselves from this wicked generation." Those who understood the truth of St. Peter's words were baptized that very same day. About three thousand souls were baptized by the apostles on that first Pentecost Sunday.

After the new Christians were baptized, they learned all they could about Christ's teachings from the apostles. When they knew their Faith well, the apostles "laid their hands upon them, and they received the Holy Spirit." This was the first Confirmation.

Bishops are the successors to the apostles. The Bishop confirms us when we are ready to receive Confirmation and the Holy Spirit comes to strengthen us with His special Gifts. We, too, like the apostles, must never be afraid to tell the truth about Jesus Christ and His Church.

Pentecost

Confirmation

Confirmation is a Sacrament through which the Holy Spirit comes to us in a special way.

Confirmation helps us to be strong, virtuous Christians and soldiers of Jesus Christ.

We need the Sacrament of Confirmation to make us strong to fight against all evils.

In Confirmation, the Holy Spirit comes to us in a special way.

Confirmation helps us to explain the Catholic Faith to our neighbors.

Confirmation helps us to practice our Catholic Faith.

Confirmation helps us to be missionaries and soldiers for Jesus Christ.

Confirmation gives us the Gifts of the Holy Spirit.

Confirmation gives us the courage to tell our neighbors about Jesus.

Confirmation gives us the strength to suffer for Jesus if necessary.

What is Confirmation?

Confirmation is the sacrament through which the Holy Spirit comes to us in a special way to make us soldiers of Jesus Christ.

How does Confirmation help us?

Confirmation helps us to be strong and brave soldiers of Jesus Christ.

Confirmation helps us to be strong and brave soldiers of Jesus Christ.

The Catholic Church

Jesus knew that when He went back to Heaven, centuries would pass while new Christians were born and baptized. Jesus gave us the Catholic Church so that all the truths He taught His apostles about the Kingdom of God would be taught to us exactly as He taught them to the apostles.

Jesus appointed Peter as the first pope and head of His Church.
Then Jesus sent the Holy Spirit to help the apostles.
The Holy Spirit filled them with Grace.
This Grace made the apostles brave and strong.

St. Peter, the First Pope

The apostles were the first bishops and priests of the Catholic Church.
The bishops and priests of the Catholic Church give us the Sacraments.
The Catholic Church gives us the Sacraments to help us get to Heaven.

Jesus gave us the Catholic Church.
He commanded Peter and the apostles to teach us about Heaven.

The pope, the bishops, and the priests teach us and help us to go to Heaven.

They teach us to know Jesus.
They help us to learn about God.
They help us to love God and obey His Commandments.
They help us to serve God and become holy and pleasing to God.

Jesus gave us the Catholic Church.

The Catholic Church

The Catholic Church is the Church which Jesus Himself gave us. Peter was made the head of the Catholic Church.

Jesus said to Peter: "You are Peter. (The name Peter means rock.) Upon this rock, Peter, I will build My Church." Jesus made Peter the first pope. The Holy Spirit made Peter strong in holiness like a rock. The pope represents Jesus and is the head of His Church on earth.

Jesus sent the Holy Spirit to help Peter and the apostles.
Jesus loves His Catholic Church.
I love the Catholic Church.
The Catholic Church gives us the Seven Sacraments.

Peter was made the head of the Catholic Church.

The Seven Sacraments of the Church are: Baptism, Penance, Holy Eucharist, Confirmation, Holy Orders, Matrimony, and Anointing of the Sick.

I have already been baptized.
I am preparing to receive the Sacraments of Penance and Holy Eucharist.
I will be confirmed when I am a little older.

If I marry, I will receive the Sacrament of Matrimony.
My parents received the Sacrament of Matrimony.

If a man wants to become a priest, he will receive the Sacrament of Holy Orders.
Our priests at church have received the Sacrament of Holy Orders.

If I become very sick or injured, and I'm in danger of death,
the priest will give me the last Sacrament, the Anointing of the Sick.

Anointing of the Sick

The Catholic Church

Jesus makes Peter pope.

The Catholic Church is like a loving mother.
We call her "Holy Mother Church" because she nourishes our souls.
Holy Mother Church nourishes our souls with the Seven Sacraments.

Jesus loves the Catholic Church.
Jesus loves the Catholic Church so much He calls her His Bride.
I love the Catholic Church because Jesus loves His Church.

Jesus gave the Catholic Church to the whole world.
The Catholic Church was started by Jesus.
Jesus wants everyone to know the truth and receive the Sacraments.

Jesus sent the Holy Spirit to help the Catholic Church.
Jesus sent the Holy Spirit to help the pope, the bishops, and the priests.
The priests of the Catholic Church give me Jesus in Holy Communion.
The priests of the Catholic Church forgive my sins in Confession.

I love the Catholic Church.
The Catholic Church teaches me how to obey the Commandments better.
The Catholic Church helps me to understand how I should be good.
I love the Catholic Church.

The Catholic Church is like a loving mother.
The Catholic Church, like a loving mother, helps me learn about God.
The Catholic Church helps me to love God.

Best of all, the Catholic Church gives me Jesus Christ Himself, my Lord and my God, in the Holy Eucharist.

Priests teach us about our Faith.

The Catholic Church

Who gave us the Catholic Church?
Jesus Christ gave us the Catholic Church.

How does Jesus help us to get to Heaven?
Jesus helps us to get to Heaven through the Catholic Church.

How does the Catholic Church help us to get to Heaven?
The Catholic Church helps us to get to Heaven through the Sacraments.

The Good Shepherd

Who was sent by Jesus Christ to help the Catholic Church?
The Holy Spirit, the third Person of the Blessed Trinity, was sent by Jesus Christ to help the Catholic Church.

What is the Catholic Church?
The Catholic Church is the union of all faithful Catholics under one head, the pope.

What do we call the head of the Catholic Church?
We call the head of the Catholic Church the pope.

Who did Jesus make the first pope?
Jesus made Peter the first pope when He said: "You are Peter, the rock, and on this rock I will build My Church."

"You are Peter, the rock."

Sacramentals

The Catholic Church has given us even more helpful ways to get to Heaven.
The Catholic Church calls them Sacramentals.
The Sacramentals are holy things that help us earn more Grace.

The Rosary is a Sacramental.
We say many Hail Marys when we say the Rosary.
We try to say the Rosary every day.
Through the Rosary, we recall the events in the lives of Jesus and Mary.

The Scapular is a Sacramental.
Scapulars were first worn only by monks and nuns.
Scapulars are part of the religious habit worn by monks and nuns.

The Church gave the people a smaller version of the Scapular.
Scapulars are worn around the neck.

Our Lady of the Rosary

Scapulars are a special sign that we love God and belong to Him.
They are cloth, and usually have a holy picture.
The Holy Catholic Church gives each blessed Scapular a special Grace.

Sacramentals are blessed objects.
The Rosary, Scapular, and Holy Water are some Sacramentals.
The Catholic Church has many Sacramentals, which give us Grace.

Sacramentals

Sacramentals are holy things we use which help us receive Grace.
We usually say special prayers with Sacramentals.
The most common Sacramentals are the Rosary and the Scapular.

Holy medals are Sacramentals also. The most famous medal is the
Miraculous Medal. So many people were cured with this medal,
it came to be called the Miraculous Medal.

St. Catherine Labouré, a holy Sister of Charity, said the Blessed
Mother appeared to her and designed the beautiful medal
of the Immaculate Conception.

Another sacramental is Holy Water. We see Holy Water at church,
but we may have Holy Water at home too. We bless ourselves with
the Sign of the Cross when we use Holy Water. We say: "In the Name
of the Father, and of the Son, and of the Holy Spirit. Amen."

Statues and pictures, after they are blessed, are Sacramentals.
We often pray in front of statues and pictures to help us think about
Jesus and Mary, and other saints.

The Coronation of Mary as Queen of Heaven

Sacramentals

Sacramentals are holy things we use which help us receive Grace.
We say special prayers when we use Sacramentals.

The devotion called the Stations of the Cross is also a Sacramental.
Look to see the Stations of the Cross on the walls on both sides of the church.
Each Station is a picture of what happened to Jesus on Good Friday.

Every Catholic church should have the Stations of the Cross.
The Stations of the Cross are prayed on Good Friday.
A priest or deacon leads the Stations of the Cross each Friday in Lent.

We may pray the Stations by ourselves any time we wish.
Many saints have written prayers to say at each Station.
You can pray your own prayers to Jesus at each Station.
The Catholic Church teaches us to say this prayer at each Station:

We adore Thee, O Christ, and we bless Thee,

Because by Thy Holy Cross, Thou hast redeemed the world.

At one of the Stations, Jesus meets His mother, Mary.
At another Station, Jesus meets Veronica, who wiped His face.

At another, Jesus talks to a group of holy women and mothers.
You may have seen someone walk and pray at each Station in church.
There are many outdoor shrines of the Stations of the Cross.
Have you visited an outdoor shrine of the Stations of the Cross?

Jesus meets His Mother, Mary.

Sacramentals

What are Sacramentals?

Sacramentals are holy things of which the Catholic Church makes use to obtain for us from God spiritual and temporal favors.

What is a temporal favor?

A temporal favor is something related to our everyday life, such as a safe trip or good weather.

What are the Sacramentals most used by Catholics?

The Sacramentals most used by Catholics are: Holy Water, blessed candles, blessed ashes, blessed palms, statues of Our Lord and the Blessed Mother, medals, rosaries, and scapulars.

Simon Stock receives the Scapular.

WEEK THIRTY-SIX: DAY 1

Please review the Catechism and the Catechism questions and answers for the first quarter.

WEEK THIRTY-SIX: Day 2

Please review the Catechism and the Catechism questions and answers for the second quarter.

The Good Shepherd

WEEK THIRTY-SIX: Day 3
Please review the Catechism and the Catechism questions and answers for the third quarter.

WEEK THIRTY-SIX: Day 4
Please review the Catechism and the Catechism questions and answers for the fourth quarter.

CONCLUSION

Dear Boys and Girls,

Those of us at Seton love you very much. We hope this catechism has helped you. We want to help your parents help you learn about Jesus Who loves each one of us so much.

We remember you and your family every day in our prayers at Mass and during the Angelus at noon.

Will you please remember Seton families in your prayers?

In the Holy Family,

The Seton Staff

The Holy Family

List of Paintings and Artists

Like our books?

You might like our program, too. Seton Home Study School offers a full curriculum program for kindergarten through 12th grade. We include daily lesson plans, answer keys, quarterly tests, and much more. Our staff of teachers and counselors is available to answer questions and offer help. We keep student records and send out diplomas that are backed by our accreditation with the Southern Association of Colleges and Schools and the Commission on International and Transregional Accreditation.

For more information about Seton Home Study School, please contact our admissions office.

Seton Home Study School
1350 Progress Drive
Front Royal, VA 22630

Phone: (540) 636-9990 • Fax: (540) 636-1602
Internet: http://www.setonhome.org • E-mail: info@setonhome.org